The
DYNAMIC
LAWS
of
HEALING

The
DYNAMIC
LAWS
of
HEALING

CATHERINE PONDER

Published by
DeVORSS & Company
P.O. Box 550, Marina del Rey, CA 90294

Library of Congress
Catalog Card Number: 66-17377

ISBN 0-87516-156-1

Printed in the United States of America

CONTENTS

Introduction . . . .

YOU HAVE HEALING POWER!

A Special Message from the Author

One of the greatest secrets you can ever learn is that you have healing power!

Perhaps you have thought of the "gift of healing" as a special power that belonged only to certain persons — the most spiritually advanced or the most brilliant in the practice of medicine, psychiatry, or chiropractic. Perhaps you have believed that there is something mysterious, even mystical, about healing. For many ages the word "healing" was associated with superstition and strange practices.

In recent times we have been hearing much about spiritual healing that results from the revival of various Biblical practices such as prayer, laying on of hands, special church rituals, and healing services. We have been hearing much about miracle medications and all the fine scientific advances that are effecting cures, as well as about the great strides being made in the field of mental health.

To all phases of the healing arts let us say, "Bless you and Godspeed!" because all healing is faith healing. All healing is divine. Recently when a patient daringly said to her doctor that she believed she had just had a spiritual healing, he smilingly asked, "What other kind is there?"

THE HEALING SECRET OF THE AGES

In spite of recent enlightenment, most people still think that their health is dependent upon some outside source — a spiritual, psychiatric, medical or chiropractic specialist. They believe this, even though these specialists invariably point out to them that all treatment is for the purpose of activating health *within* them.

Most people have not yet learned the healing secret of the ages — that health is basically an inside job, mentally as well as physically. No matter how successful a treatment is in time of illness, a person often becomes sick again and again, because he has not gotten at the *cause* of his illness — ill thoughts and feelings about himself, others, his Creator, and the world in which he lives. These ill thoughts constrict the life force within him, causing dis-ease, or lack of ease.

It is very interesting to realize that the word "ill" means "evil, wrong, disagreeable, incorrect." It is literally your evil, wrong, disagreeable, incorrect thoughts and feelings, located right within your body, that play such havoc with your health. The Greek physician, Hippocrates, who is known as the father of medicine, wrote around 400 B.C.: "Men ought to know that from the brain and from the brain only arise our pleasures, laughter, and jests, as well as our sorrows, pains, griefs, and fears." One of the secret teachings of the ancient Egyptians was that a pained body was the result of pained thinking. This still seems to be a secret to many people today.

HOW THESE LAWS WERE BORN

In this book I wish to share with you some of the laws of healing that deal with the *cause* of ill thoughts and feelings. More than just analyzing the cause of disease, these healing laws show you how to "turn on" the right thoughts and feelings from deep within your own being, thereby changing the whole pattern of your thinking and consequently your health.

These healing laws have been known and practiced to some degree by people down through the ages. Often they have been a secret teaching, though in recent times they have been revealed and used to some extent by the various healing arts. However, in most instances, they have been learned and used in a spasmodic, trial-and-error way only.

Several decades ago, when I came into the ministry, I quickly discovered that, like the priest-physician of ancient times, I was expected to know and use the laws of healing for helping those whom I served.

It was out of a searching sense of uncertainty about the exact laws of healing that I began to pray: "Dear God, You called me into the ministry. If You wish me to follow in the healing phases of this work, please teach me the laws of healing. Reveal them to me in a simple way so that I may share them with all mankind." This book is the answer to that prayer. It is the result of much that has been revealed, observed, learned during this period; I also invite you to read my companion books, *The Prosperity Secrets of the Ages*, and *The Healing Secrets of the Ages*, which are filled with healing secrets as well.

I have discovered that healing is constantly taking place in the lives of people in simple ways that seem miraculous; that all persons have healing power, if they but knew it! Those to whom it happens may hesitate to talk about their healing experiences, since the public still tends to feel that this type of healing may be a strange experience that comes only to "strange" people.

This book is filled with the healing accounts of people of various races, creeds, nationalities, faiths, in all walks of life, who have quietly shared with me their healing experiences and *how* they feel those healings occurred. Sometimes their healing came in conjunction with spiritual, medical, chiropractic or psychiatric help. Sometimes they did not. Regardless—these people realized they had healing power; that it was easier to "turn on" than most people think.

As I listened I realized that over and over, those healings seemed to come through the use of certain mental and spiritual laws. Herein you will find these healing laws described in an orderly sequence. They can be practiced by anyone anywhere, and in conjunction with other help being obtained.

THE FIRST STEP TOWARD HEALING

As a first step toward healing, let us analyze this book's title: *The Dynamic Laws of Healing*.

The word "dynamic" has the same root as the word "dynamite." That which is dynamic is powerful, forceful, filled with energy, and leads to change. As pointed out to me by the stockbroker who named my first book — *The Dynamic Laws of Prosperity*—that which is dynamic tends to blast you out of a rut!

A "law" is a principle that works. Sir William Blackstone, well-known writer of the law, pointed out more than two hundred years ago, that a "law" is a settled rule of action. The word "law" usually suggests a desire for order. People in ill health need just that—*order* in their thinking, emotions, bodies, and lives.

We would agree with the brilliant scientist, Sir Isaac Newton, an early explorer of nature's laws, that there is one set of natural laws for the physical world. But let us go further: There are also higher mental and spiritual laws than those usually used on the physical plane of life. Jesus knew and used them constantly. These higher mental and spiritual laws are so powerful that they can be used to multiply natural laws, neutralize natural laws, or even reverse natural laws! It is when these higher mental and spiritual laws are invoked through the mind of man, that they often produce results that seem miraculous on the physical plane. It is then that the "impossible" becomes possible, the "incurable" becomes curable, and miracle healings occur.

As Plato pointed out to the Greek physicians of his time, the word "health" means a state of being *whole, hearty, sound in all phases of your being—spirit, soul, body, affairs.* Health includes healthy financial affairs; healthy relationships with others; a healthy spiritual understanding.

When these dynamic laws of healing are invoked, they can do just what the title implies—produce dynamic, forceful changes which lead to orderly results in mind, body, and affairs. A new state of wholeness can develop. Thereafter, the user finds these laws a fine preventive medicine, too.

Not only can you use these ideas to help activate wholeness within yourself, but you can use them to help others to a greater realization of health.

HOW THESE LAWS HAVE HELPED OTHERS

A doctor once told me that he had shocked many people into healing as he pointed out the truth about God, man, and the universe to them. The shock caused them to release old negative thought patterns, opening the way for new life and vitality to well up within them. These shocking truths about healing are found in Chapter 1 of this book.

A businessman was healed of a heart condition, from which he was supposed to die, as he used the "no" law for healing described in Chapter 2. A housewife used this same law for her husband's healing of cancer, after he had been sent home from the hospital to die. Instead of dying, he recovered.

Upon discovering a lump in her breast, a housewife felt led to quietly invoke the "surprise" law of healing (Chapter 3). A month later, she received another surprise — when she realized that the lump was gone. She never knew when it disappeared.

A housewife was healed of leukemia after practicing the healing law of release (Chapter 4). A middle-aged woman conquered menopause and went through the change of life victoriously; a businessman stopped smoking; and a retired sea captain healed himself of alcoholism—as each one used the "yes" law of healing (Chapter 5).

An elderly woman gradually but completely recovered from painful "incurable" arthritis through using the healing law of love (Chapter 7). A businessman was healed of paralysis; another of rheumatism and heart trouble, after each invoked the miracle law of healing (Chapter 8). A college dean recovered from a lingering nervous breakdown as she used the occult law of healing (Chapter 9). An incurable skin condition was cleared up after the imaging law of healing was practiced by a young girl and her mother (Chapter 10).

Many other happy instances could be cited. Instead, I suggest you go quickly to the following pages of this book, where you will find the various healing laws, and the happy results they have brought to others, fully explained.

You can immediately begin learning and applying these dynamic laws of healing as forces for bringing wholeness to you!

Catherine Ponder
P.O. Drawer 1278
Palm Desert, California 92261
U.S.A.

THE SHOCKING TRUTH
ABOUT HEALING

— Chapter 1 —

The shocking truth about healing is that *you* have healing power within you. The word "health" comes from an Anglo-Saxon word meaning "hale," "whole," "well," and "hearty." This should be your condition at all times. If it is not, there is something you can do about it — *now!*

Though you are unaware of it, your healing power is quietly at work within you at all times repairing cells, carrying off wastes, nourishing tissues, and healing wounds.

Occasionally this healing power reveals itself in some remarkable way: someone is critically ill, not expected to live. Suddenly, with no explanation, the growth vanishes, the wound heals, or the heart restores itself. This proves that the human body is undoubtedly the most powerful self-sufficient dynamo in existence for the carrying on of life!

This inner power of healing is not an extraordinary one. It is a natural part of your inner world. Twenty-four hours a day it is supervising all the fantastically complicated operations of your body. In a single cell, the super-scientist in you effortlessly performs functions that the world's most accomplished chemists cannot duplicate. Much of this healing power is carried on through the automatic functions of your subconscious mind.

However, you can begin to release this healing power within you in deeper degrees, as and when needed, through the power of your deliberate, conscious thinking. As you do, the power of your thought moves through both your conscious and subconscious mind activities, putting you on the road to health again.

The fact that you have this healing power within you, which you can deliberately release through your thinking, does not mean that you should not avail yourself of the usual methods of help. Instead, it means that the ideas set forth in this book can help hasten your complete healing, in conjunction with other methods employed. The sixteenth-century German physician, Paracelsus, said: "The curative power of medicines often consist not so much in the spirit that is hidden in them, as in the spirit in which they are taken." May this book set you in that right spirit.

THE CAUSE OF DISEASE

The reason you have healing power within you which you can begin to consciously release is this: *The*

*body has a superwisdom within it that is biased toward
health, rather than toward disease.*

This life force in man has been estimated to be at
least ten times more powerful than any form of treatment he may take, though various treatments are
helpful in releasing this inner force.

Since the body is filled with such amazing restorative
powers, why is man ever sick?

The shocking truth is that disease is self-inflicted!
Disease is caused by wrong thoughts, opinions, and beliefs, moving upon and within the body, constricting
the life force. "Envy, hate, and fear, when these senti-
ments are habitual, are capable of starting organic
changes and genuine disease," wrote scientist-doctor
Alexis Carrel[1] decades ago. Within recent times, his
professional colleagues have begun to agree. When
you change those negative beliefs and emotions, you
change the body which house them in its cells.

Dr. Phineas P. Quimby proved these ideas in the
1800's effecting thousands of cures in his New England
neighbors. Because of his success, he became known as
the founder of mental and spiritual healing in America,[2] and a number of people who studied his theories
formed healing movements of their own, through
which countless thousands have been helped.

MIND POWER IN EVERY CELL

The shocking truth is that the mind isn't located only
in the brain, as most of us have been led to believe.
The mind is found in every cell of your body. When

---

1. *Man the Unknown*, Harper & Bros., N.Y. 1935.
2. *The Quimby Manuscripts*, edited by Horatio W. Dresser,
The Julian Press, Inc., N.Y. 1961.

you pinch your arm, it is the brain cells within your flesh that feel that pressure and respond, "Ouch!"

Similar ideas gather themselves together and become "thought centers." These centers settle in various parts of the body, affecting the body according to their positive or negative nature. Every cell is enveloped in thought. As Edison discovered, "Every cell 'thinks'." Scientists state it more technically by saying that every cell is filled with life, light, intelligence and substance, which form an atomic structure.

Charles Fillmore, a Kansas City realtor, discovered the dynamic power that thought has on the body at the turn of the century. He used it to heal himself of painful tuberculosis of the hip, from which he had suffered since childhood. In his book, *Atom Smashing Power of Mind*,[3] he not only describes his healing, but explains the power that thought has on the body, explaining that states of mind established in consciousness gather to themselves vitamins, cells, nerves, muscles, and flesh itself. He felt that in the mind, man can generate every medicine that is necessary for the upbuilding and restoring of the body. He stated that you can literally rebuild your body cell by cell by rebuilding your thinking. By renewal of your mind, your body can be transformed, since your body is the visible record of your thoughts. *As a man thinks in his mind, so is he in his body.*

THE BODY IS NOT SOLID

If the body were a solid mass of flesh and bone, it might be difficult to believe that the mind has this

_____
3. Published by Unity Books, Unity Village, MO, 1949.

much power over it; but there is nothing solid in the body; it is about 80 percent water. Though we often think of the bones as a hard mass, in reality they are filled with a fluid substance and are soft, pliable and porous. The reason for this is that they are penetrated by the capillaries of the blood, as the blood corpuscles are formed within the bones. If that which appears solid in the body were condensed into actual solids, your body would not be as big as a fly speck!

Because of its fluid content, thoughts move easily in and through the body to reshape it—to build it up or tear it down, according to the nature of man's thinking. *The strongest thing in your body is your thinking! The body is soft, pliable, and even plastic to your thoughts.*

WHY NEGATIVE THINKERS MAY BE HEALTHY

If the body is so strongly affected by one's thoughts, why is it that some negative thinkers still seem to enjoy good health?

The reason is this: The body is much slower in recording thoughts of evil than those of good, since its true office is to produce life and health. In fact, one healthy thought persistently expressed can nullify 1,000 unhealthy thoughts.

Since its super-wisdom is biased toward health instead of toward illness, the body tries, and often is able, to throw off man's negative thinking for a long time. It is his *habitual* wrong thoughts, deep hates, secret resentments, and strong prejudices that play such havoc with his health. Invariably, those people who persist in such negative emotions suffer a diseased result in mind, body or affairs, whether you are aware of their distress or not.

It is the negative emotions of long standing that must be cleared out of the conscious and subconscious levels of the mind in order to relieve serious health problems. Just as man did not acquire these negative concepts overnight, he often is not able to release them overnight; and he should not be impatient as he works to clear them up.

HOW TO RELEASE HEALING POWER

People constantly prove that the body is pliable and plastic to their thinking, in both positive and negative ways.

A civil service employee worked in an office where everyone was suffering from colds and flu. Instead of entertaining this possibility for herself, this employee began affirming: "I AM LETTING DIVINE INTELLIGENCE EXPRESS PERFECTION THROUGH ME NOW." These words recognized and released the super-intelligence within her body, and she remained healthy.

A businessman attended a lecture in an air-conditioned ballroom. Sitting near him was a lady who kept complaining that the room was too cool, and that she would get a sore throat. As she fed the intelligence within her body this idea, it responded by producing a scratchy throat for her before the hour had passed.

The businessman would not accept this idea, though in the past he had often suffered the same symptoms under similar conditions. Having learned that he could release healing power through his thoughts, he began silently decreeing: "I AM DIVINE INTELLIGENCE.

EVERY PART OF MY BODY IS FILLED WITH DIVINE INTELLI-
GENCE. I AM WHOLE, WELL, HARMONIOUS THROUGH AND
THROUGH." He remained well.

Your body, as fluid substance, is filled with mind
power. This fluid substance feeds your thoughts. When
you entertain uplifted thoughts, it sometimes surprises
you how fast your body responds with good health.

A schoolteacher in England read my book, *The Prosperity Secrets of the Ages*, and from it learned that the
body is composed of radiant substance. This idea fascinated her. She had long suffered from cracked finger-
nails, presumably the result of the chalk she used daily
in her classroom, for which she had found no remedy.
As she meditated often upon the idea that her finger-
nails were radiant substance, they immediately improved and soon were normal again.

Do not deprecate your body. There are those who
ignorantly say that the body is evil and unimportant, a
mere shadow of the real person which it houses. Like
the Apostle Paul, realize that your body is the temple
of the living God, and that you should glorify God in it
as radiant health. (I Corinthians 6:19,20)

HEALING IS GOD'S WILL

Perhaps you've heard people self-righteously say: "I
guess it is God's will for me to be sick, so I must endure this pain." What a neurotic God such people are
worshipping—a God made in *their* limited image and
likeness!

If these people truly believed it was God's will for
them to suffer, they would never go to a doctor or take
any other constructive action toward healing.

Though such people usually consider themselves "good Christians," they consistently overlook the fact that God sent His son to perform most of the Biblical miracles for restoring the sick. If God considered illness a blessing, why do that? And why did He allow His son to promise His followers, which include modern-day Christians: "He that believeth on me, the works that I do shall he do also; and greater works than these shall he do." (John 14:12)

God does not send suffering to purify you for a future life in heaven. *You do not have to go through hell here to get to heaven hereafter.* The word "heaven" means "harmony," and when you get into harmony with yourself, your fellow men, and your Creator, you are well on the way to manifesting a heavenly state of health here and now, thus fulfilling the prophet John's promise, "The kingdom of heaven is at hand." (Matthew 3:2)

HOW RELIGION RELATES TO HEALTH

A supposedly "good Christian" was asked to attend a ten-day spiritual retreat. Hesitantly she accepted the invitation. As she was packing for the trip, her husband said, "Honey, *try* to enjoy yourself. *Try* to have a good time."

"At a spiritual retreat?" she retorted.

Bracing herself for the experience, she prayed that she would be able to "stand spiritual things for ten days." However, she had such a good time at the retreat that she has been attending them regularly ever since, and enjoying them thoroughly.

Many people are like this lady: They have a false idea of what it is like to be a "good Christian" because they have a false idea of the true nature of God whom they worship. They consider God as having a split personality of good and evil; they consider Him a distant entity who punishes them severely, perhaps through ill health for their every misdeed.

Their misguided negative beliefs about their Creator set up a chain reaction of negative thinking about themselves and the world about them. Their attitudes take on this negation in the form of self-righteousness, piety, condemnation, and resentment of all who do not conform to their beliefs. These negative attitudes are the reason why so many "good Christians" suffer illness and then blame their diseased conditions on God, rather than on their own diseased thinking.

In reality, the so-called righteous are often afflicted with ill health, because they see more faults in mankind than any other class of people! As for their pious fault-finding, according to the noted Viennese psychologist, Alfred Adler, piety is an unhealthy form of neurosis, rather than a healthy form of religion. Having encountered many pious, unhealthy neurotics in his work, one theologian has knowingly spoken of the "odor of piety." Still another theologian has bluntly said, " 'Saints' are all right in heaven, but they are hell on earth!"

The word "religion" literally means "to bind back," or to relink you to your Source. Your religion is for the purpose of binding you back to God, and His goodness. Since God is a loving Father, who wills only supreme good for you, then to be bound back to Him is to be bound back to life, health, vitality, and to nothing less. God is a God of health! What is not well with you cannot possibly be the will of God.

GOODNESS HAS NOTHING TO DO WITH IT

A famous actress showed a gift of expensive jewelry to a friend who exclaimed, "My goodness!" Quipped the actress: "Goodness had nothing to do with it."

Goodness has nothing to do with your ill health either. Any evidence of disease in the body is an evidence of *un*holiness in mind. *You will never be sick because of your goodness!* Disease is just the opposite, a lack of ease, a lack of goodness.

FOOLISH BELIEFS ABOUT ILLNESS

People have long attributed ill health to everything but its true cause: their own wrong thoughts and feelings.

In 1720 the Black Death plague hit Europe. The Spanish clergy said it was the result of opera-attendance. The English bishops blamed it on theater-going. Other clergymen said it was caused by the fashionable, long, pointed shoes the people wore, which irritated God. Still others claimed the plague was the result of corruption in politics.

"Ridiculous," you say. Yet in this enlightened age, we still entertain beliefs that are just as foolish and just as harmful to our health.

There are a number of erroneous religious beliefs about God and man that cause sickness. Indeed, religious beliefs have a very vital or a very devitalizing effect upon the mind and body. If you believe you are a worm of the dust, you can hardly claim your spiritual heritage of health. A belief in Satan often makes people ill. A belief in the end of the world by fire and brimstone makes others sick.

A doctor once told me he always had his largest number of patients when a nearby church held "revival" meetings. A patient appeared one morning complaining of intense pain. Upon examining her, he found no physical cause for her suffering. Close questioning revealed that the pain had begun the night before while she was attending a "revival" meeting at the nearby church. As the minister had described at length his belief in the hell and brimstone future that awaited all who did not come forth to be saved at the conclusion of the service, this lady became aware of pain in her body, which remained with her throughout the night and into the following day. Her doctor suggested she revise her ideas about God, dwelling more upon His goodness, if she wished to avail herself of a pain-free existence.

Revivals are needed, but only those which revive the ideas of God's goodness and its availability to man. I trust that, as you read this book, you will find yourself attending such a "revival."

HEALTH AND SALVATION ARE THE SAME

The Hebrew and Greek words translated "salvation" and "health" in the Bible are often the same.

Permanent health comes from freeing the mind of its beliefs in ignorance and sin, rather than adding to that belief. Right thinking is the greatest form of salvation, and it leads to good health.

Plato told the Greek physicians of his time that the cause of their failure to heal lay in their ignorance of the needs of the soul. If Plato were alive today, he would probably make the same statement to those members of the clergy who try to frighten, rather than inspire, their followers into the kingdom.

Actually, the kingdom of heaven begins as a state of mind here and now—a heavenly state of mind. When you save yourself from negative thinking, you not only save your soul from disease but also your body which houses the soul.

THE DIFFERENCE BETWEEN CURING AND HEALING

Although man is only about 2 percent physical and 98 percent mental and spiritual, the average person spends about 98 percent of his time thinking about the 2 percent of his physical nature! That is why he often suffers ill health. He is trying to attain good health from without-in, rather than from within-out.

Plato told the Greek physicians: "The part can never be well unless the whole is well." There is a difference between "healing" and "curing" a person, as Plato realized from the above statement. To "heal" is to "make whole" the entire man—spirit, soul and body. To "cure" means to "eliminate or relieve immediate distress." A person is often cured of pain by seeking medical treatment. But unless he changes his negative thought patterns that cause the pain, it may appear again and again, either in the same area or in another part of the body.

Psychologists have found that most disease is self-inflicted. A sense of guilt finds atonement in illness: when the mind does not get relief from guilt, it releases the guilt into the body as disease. Disease in the body is actually the body's attempt to throw off ill feelings. When you feel ill, it is because your ill feelings are trying to get away from you! Thus, it is worth the time and effort involved to change your thought patterns, freeing them of guilt, in order to effect a complete healing, rather than experiencing only a temporary cure, which technical treatment alone may bring.

WHY MANY PEOPLE ARE CONFUSED

For 300 years after Jesus Christ, there were great works of healing performed among His followers. Then slowly the ministry of healing ceased as the church became more prosperous and worldly.

It had become a sign of spiritual power to be able to heal, and some people not high in the church could heal better than those who were. This aroused jealousy. The ministry of healing was then forbidden, first among high church officials, then among laymen.

As spiritual healing subsided, the practice of healing through medicine became popular with the masses, since it did not demand the faith required by spiritual healing.

Later, antagonism arose between the church and the medical profession. In 529 A.D. the Emperor Justinian closed the medical schools of Athens and Alexandria as a gesture of churchly disapproval. This disapproval of physicians on the part of the church continued for many centuries, though here and there in monasteries medical manuscripts were copied. In 1215 Pope Innocent the Third condemned surgery and all who practiced it. In 1428 the dissection of the body was pronounced sacrilegious and the study of the anatomy was condemned.

It is little wonder that many people have been so confused in their religious beliefs concerning the church's stand on healing since, for many centuries, the church waged a feud with the medical profession, as well as within its own gates, even to the extent of forbidding spiritual healing.

The Swiss psychologist Dr. Carl Jung has said, "Healing may be called a religious problem." In these times, more and more thinking people agree with him and are returning to a practice of first-century Christianity, which was filled with healing power, and which promised healing power to all true believers.

ANCIENT HEBREWS KNEW THE SECRET

There is nothing new about the power of the mind over the body. Had the ancient Babylonian sciences come down to us intact, our civilization might be even more advanced than it is. Not only did the Babylonians use strange stones of ore for curing cancer (probably radium), but they were also experts in the use of psychosomatics, various mental techniques, and even hypnotism. They also practiced what is known today as "holistic medicine," or healing of the whole person.

It is believed that Abraham, who grew up in the Babylonian city of Ur, learned of their use of psychosomatics and brought it to the Jews. In any event, the

Hebrews looked upon disease as a result of sin or of making mistakes. But they did not feel they had to tolerate disease.

The first healing recorded in the Bible, in the time of Abraham, reflects this ancient teaching about health. King Abimelech had taken Abraham's wife, Sarah, thinking her to be Abraham's sister. In a dream the Lord advised him to return Sarah to Abraham, because she was his wife. The Lord promised that if the King did not do so, he and his family would die.

When King Abimelech did return Sarah, "Abraham prayed unto God, and God healed Abimelech and his wife and his maid-servants; and they bore children. For Jehovah had fast closed up all the wombs of the house of Abimelech, because of Sarah, Abraham's wife." (Genesis 20:17,18)

This passage clearly shows that wrong thought, feeling and action had caused sterility in King Abimelech, his wife, and his maid-servants. Right thought, feeling and action, accompanied by prayer, restored fertility.

Moses later pointed out in his writings the definite power of right attitudes and emotional responses for health, and the power of wrong ones for ill health; when his sister, Miriam, criticized him for marrying into another race (Numbers 12:1), the Bible states that Miriam contracted leprosy, and was healed only by means of Moses' prayer. Criticism of one's self, and of others, is still a major factor in ill health.

GERMS: A RESULT

While modern physicians accredit Hipprocrates with being the Father of Medicine, the ancients felt that the immortal Hermes was the founder of healing. From the scholarly Hermes, they derived the secret Hermetic teaching. Those teachings contained some of the great truths that are now being rediscovered as psychosomatic medicine.

For instance, they felt that one of the primary causes of disease was unhealthy, abnormal mental attitudes: depression, morbid emotions, excessive hate, resentment, condemnation of one's self, criticism of others, jealousy, and possessiveness. They felt that such unhealthy thinking resulted in ulcers, tumors, cancers, fevers, tuberculosis, paralysis, and all types of nervous conditions. Furthermore, the ancients considered germs as a creation of man's evil thoughts and actions. *Germs were a result, not a cause, they maintained.*

After ancient times, for many centuries, people knew nothing about germs. Finally, during the Middle Ages, an Italian nobleman, Hieronymus Fracastorius, again formulated the theory of germs, and nobody believed him! This nobleman was so ridiculed for his germ theory that he finally gave up the idea. Several centuries elapsed before two men, Leeuwenhoek and Pasteur, reconfirmed his theory.

In the book, *Atom Smashing Power of Mind*, Charles Fillmore gives a modern metaphysician's viewpoint on germs, which agrees with the ancient Hermetic germ-theory:

> The physician takes it for granted that disease germs exist as an integral part of the natural world. The metaphysician sees disease germs as the manifested result of anger, revenge, jealousy, fear, impure thinking and many other mind activities. Disease germs, created and named by the intellect of man, have

enough intelligence to come when they are called. A change of mind will change the character of the germ. Love, courage, peace, strength, and good will form good character and build bodily structures of a nature like the qualities of the mind.

YOUR HEALING CHORD

Doctors have said that 75 percent of us are using only 25 percent of our physical powers; that we are only half alive. Compared with what we might be, we are pygmies physically, when we might be giants, enjoying gigantic good health.

The dynamic energy you can release through the right use of your conscious thought is very great. Since your thoughts are constantly changing your body, your deliberate thoughts can deliberately change your body from disease to health.

There is always one chord in every mind that is capable of responding promptly to the healing idea. It is when this healing chord is not struck that people continue in their sickness.

Take the ideas in this book that excite you and delight you. Practice them over and over. Through them you can find and strike your healing chord. As you do, you will know what Isaiah meant when he promised: "Then shall thy light break forth as the morning, and thy healing shall spring forth speedily." (Isaiah 58:8)

THE "NO" LAW OF HEALING

Chapter 2

A famous comedian was informed by his doctor, "Your illness is all in your mind." Quipped the comedian, "What a place for it to be!"

It may seem that your body and your circumstances control your thoughts, but quite the opposite is true. Your thoughts control your body and your circumstances.

As a man thinks in his mind, so is he in his body.

A medical journal once related an incident showing the power that thought has on the body:

A doctor diagnosed the cases of two men who applied to him for help. He was to let them know the result next day by letter. He wrote to one that he was free from disease, but told the other that his condition was very serious; that by going to the mountains he might

25

prolong his life for a time, but that his heart was bad and he would eventually die.

By mistake the letters were misdirected, and the healthy young man received the one containing the word that his case was hopeless. Immediately he gave up his work and went to the mountains, where, in a short time he died. The patient for whom this diagnosis was intended received instead the word that he was perfectly healthy, and in a short time he was the picture of health.

DISEASE IS SELF-INFLICTED

As previously stated, the shocking truth about disease is that it is self-inflicted! You inflict disease upon yourself by your fears, resentments, hates, and beliefs in evil. The Hindu scriptures described it: "If a man speaks or acts with an evil thought, pain follows him."

For instance, thoughts of fear release hormones into the bloodstream that can even paralyze the vital nerve centers of the body. Extreme fear actually cooks the corpuscles of the blood. Also, experiments have shown that telling a lie involves real work for the body. Your metabolism, pulse rate, blood pressure, and respiration speed up when you fib — and your eyes tend to get shifty. This is how false thinking affects the body!

Negative appearances in the body are built up and sustained by someone feeling badly about them. *What you fear, you multiply.* You build up and keep alive the diseased appearance by feeding it the substance of your negative thoughts. When the bad feeling is removed, the diseased appearance starves for lack of at-

tention and nourishment. It has to fade away because
it has nothing to sustain it.

MAN BY-PASSES THE TREE OF LIFE

In the Garden of Eden allegory, we find the secret
for health or lack of it:

In the beginning God created man perfect and gave
him dominion over everything upon the earth, including his health. But man did not appreciate his
healthy heritage. He deliberately partook of the tree
of "knowledge of good and evil," thereby dwelling
upon evil and subjecting himself to its reaction upon
his body.

His heritage of health could have been restored because there was a second tree in the Garden—the tree
of life. But by partaking of the fruit of the first tree,
and thereby deliberately dwelling upon the thought of
evil, man was prevented from eating of the fruit of the
tree of life. Through that symbolic act, man subjected
himself to evil and its attendant diseased conditions in
his body.

It is an allegory that applies in modern times as well.
When you behold the good, you are powerful, but the
instant you behold evil, you are paralyzed by the darkness of your mind. Evil has no life, substance or intelligence of itself. It is conjured up by the limited beliefs
of man. Evil is a form of darkness that flees in the presence of light—and enlightenment.

That enlightenment comes as you remind yourself
that no evil condition, however trying, is everlasting.
Such an experience is actually one in which evil is coming to the surface to be freed and released forever. Evil

wants to be released from its negation. It wants to be transmuted into good. Thus, *it will always move on!* A new condition then arises and a new, happier cycle always follows.

All the power that evil seems to have, has been given it by man, and man alone can withdraw that power. That man has this power — to deny and dissolve all disintegrating, discordant, and disease-forming ideas of evil; and to transmute apparent evil into good — is among the greatest discoveries of all ages!

THE FIRST LAW OF HEALING

Denial is the first law of healing.

Through the use of denial, you withdraw from your mind the negative beliefs and emotions that have played such havoc in your health. Denial is the first practical step toward wiping out of your mind the mistaken beliefs of a lifetime. *What you believe in, you serve and are served by.* As you change wrong beliefs, you will find a change taking place in your troublesome circumstances and bodily conditions. Scientists have long been at a loss to explain why man's body should ever be sick or die, if it were properly fed and *cleansed.* Denial cleanses your mind and body of the belief in evil, and its consequent dire physical effects.

The word "deny" not only means to "withhold," "erase," "eliminate," "dissolve," "withdraw," but it also means to "declare not to be true that which appears true." Through using the healing law of denial, you begin to erase beliefs from your mind, and evil appearances from your body.

Through denial you can also go a step further, and declare not to be true the pain, inharmony and disease that may still appear for a time. As you deny them power, you rob those appearances of any permanent life, and they fade away from neglect.

Through the act of denial, you do not deny the existence of the adverse condition, nor do you hesitate to seek technical treatment for a cure. But, along with this, you also begin to go deep within your thinking and recognize the adversity for what it is: A diseased appearance, created by your own diseased thinking. You then do something about it; you deny your wrong thoughts that brought it into existence. It is then you learn the truth of that age-old axiom: *"If you can put a thing out of your mind, you can put it out of your body."*

HOW TO USE YOUR "NO" POWER

Since denial dissolves, eliminates, erases, frees, it is your "no" power for healing.

Any thought, statement or prayer that helps you to say, "NO, I DO NOT ACCEPT THIS APPEARANCE AS NECESSARY OR LASTING IN MY LIFE," is a denial. Many a case has been healed when someone mentally said, "No, no, no," while people were talking of the ills involved.

You can free yourself from all sorts of troubles when you begin to say "no" to them, instead of continuing to dwell upon them. A seriously sprained ankle was completely healed overnight when the one suffering kept saying, "no," to the pain. During the night when the pain tried to reappear the one using denial would say,

"IT SIMPLY CANNOT BE. IT IS NOT SO. I DO NOT ACCEPT
THIS CONDITION. IT IS NOTHING. IT HAS NO POWER." Her
words proved true.

Occultists have long described denial as the law of
"divine indifference." The ancients spoke of denial as
your everlasting "no" power, pointing out that as you
used your "no" power on situations that troubled you,
they could not last, because denial dissolves, eliminates, frees. By declaring, "No, no, no," you send into
mind and body a force that shatters fixed states of
mind, which have caused disease. If true denials were
more often made, health would spring forth naturally.
Bodily functions have a way of righting themselves
when you correct the negative states of mind that caused them. Cases of swelling, tumors, and fevers, have
disappeared when someone said "no" to them.

*Use your everlasting "no" power on situations and
conditions you do not want to last.*

HOW SHE OVERCAME MORNING SICKNESS

A secretary knew the power of saying "no" to conditions she did not wish to last. Upon learning she was
to have her first baby, this young wife decided she
wished to continue working as long as possible, and
that ill health was not a necessary part of pregnancy.

When "morning sickness" began, she said to a fellow
worker, "This is ridiculous. There is no reason for me
to suffer. Having a baby is a normal process for the
body. Tomorrow I shall remain at home and straighten
out my thinking. I refuse to accept this 'morning
sickness' as necessary or lasting."

The next day she remained at home, using the healing power of denial. She mentally said, "No," to any suggestion of nausea and freed her mind of the belief that discomfort was a necessary part of pregnancy. The following day this secretary returned to work and continued on the job until a few weeks before her baby was born. A healthy pregnancy and later, a healthy child, was the result.

ALL PEOPLE NEED DENIAL

There are also people who turn away from denial, considering it an unpleasant word. They haughtily say, "I do not use the healing law of denial. *I* do not need it." Such misguided souls are usually the ones who need it most! *Everyone needs to use the healing law of denial, because everyone has negative beliefs that need to be dissolved.* The ancients believed that there were seven layers of negation in the mind of man that stood between him and his good, and that these could be continually cleansed through "no" attitudes of mind. Biblical symbology substantiates this belief through the story of the leper, Naaman, who was healed after following Elisha's instruction to wash in the Jordan River seven times. (II Kings 5:10)

Don't be afraid of the word "denial." It does not mean the foregoing of comforts and the good things of life. It does not mean to make one's self miserable by "giving up" anything of value. True denial is a letting go of the lesser to make room for the greater. Denial is a mental process by which you surrender all the old

ghosts of fear, worry, sorrow, sickness, sin, and suffering, that have haunted you, and kept your good from
you. These ghosts were figments of your imagination.
Through denial you cleanse them from your conscious
and subconscious phases of mind, perhaps without
even realizing just what they are.

As you cleanse your mind of negative beliefs, you
withhold the substance of your thoughts from them.
You disrobe them, rob them of their power, and their
very existence.

AFFIRMATIONS CANNOT REPLACE DENIAL

There are those who claim that the healing law of
affirmation, as described in Chapter 5, is sufficient.
To argue that affirmation fulfills the law of demonstration, without *first* using denial is foolish — as foolish as
the maid who thinks she has cleaned house, when she
has merely opened the windows to let the sunshine
stream in, without ever having dusted or in any way
cleaned the house's interior. How unsightly that house
would be, without this necessary "denial!"

To mentally affirm a healthy condition, without
first denying and destroying the negative emotions that
caused your ill health, is like attempting to build a new
house on a site already occupied by an old building.

*Before your problems can be resolved, there must be
a mental and emotional housecleaning.* The healing
laws of denial, forgiveness and release, as found in this
and the next two chapters, are offered you for that
purpose.

Since this book was first written several decades ago,
the author has received numerous reports of healings

that were experienced by people through their study and application of the healing laws described in this and the next two chapters. These reports, some of even supposedly "incurable" conditions, indicate the surprising power for healing that lies in the consistent use of denial, forgiveness and release!

WHEN AFFIRMATIONS DO NOT HEAL

A businesswoman had had a house for rent for months. Needing the rental income to help put her children through college, she diligently had made affirmation upon affirmation for its rental. Nothing happened. Upon learning of the "no" power of the mind she realized why her affirmations had not worked —they had not cleared her mind of fearful anxiety. Thereafter, when the subject of this unrented house popped into her mind, she would say to herself, "NO, NO, NO. THERE IS NOTHING TO FEAR. THE PERFECT TENANTS NOW APPEAR AND RENT THIS HOUSE." Though months of affirmations had rendered no results, within three days of her use of denials, the house was rented!

A worried mother wrote, "I cannot understand it. For months I have been using affirmations for my daughter and her family, and things have only gotten worse. She has been mentally ill. Her psychiatric treatments seem ineffective. Her husband's job is threatened. The children have all been sick. Recently, a fire occurred in the house. There has been constant confusion and irritation. Why haven't affirmations helped this situation?"

When this woman learned of the healing power of denial, she realized why. Affirmations make firm. To say affirmations in the midst of inharmony is to "make firm" or say "yes" to the false beliefs that cause that inharmony—this only invites more confusion into the situation! This lady proved it.

As she immediately began to say, "No, no, no" to the troubled appearances, it was like a healing balm that began clearing out the fear, inharmony, confusion. The daughter regained her emotional balance. The son-in-law was led to a better job. The children's health improved. The insurance company made a settlement on the fire in the home, that made it possible to redecorate the entire house—a desire of long standing fulfilled. Peace gradually came into this family group, after one interested person began to say "no" to the previous difficulties.

YOU MUST BE EMPHATIC   .

When you are trying to meet a hard condition, you cannot gently tap at it with your thoughts, words, and prayers, and expect to achieve a satisfying result.

You must do something more definite, more emphatic. *Ancient philosophers found that hard conditions could be completely broken up and dissolved through extensive use of denial. You can use denials and dissolve your hardest trials, because denials contain a cleansing, freeing power.*

Nothing straightens out the mind like looking all claims of evil boldly in the face with the denial, "NO, NO, NO. IT IS NOT SO. YOU HAVE NO POWER. YOU ARE NOTHING. GET THEE HENCE." *Not believing in evil takes the sting out of evil. When you remove evil's sting, you also remove its power!*

HOW DENIAL HEALED A HEART CONDITION

After years of hard work, a businessman suffered a series of heart attacks. When his doctor intimated that he could not live, his wife telephoned for prayers. Both he and his wife refused to believe he would die as they busily invoked the healing power of denial.

One night in great pain, he weakly raised up from his hospital bed and in verbal prayer said, "Lord, this is it. I've had enough pain. I refuse to remain in this condition. With Your help, I am going to get well." To the continuing pain he silently said, "No, no, no."

That night proved to be the turning point. He recovered and resumed a normal life, as he took a less strenuous job, and moved with his family to another town. There he went on to greater business success and better health than ever before.

Several years later, a relative met this man's former doctor, who asked, "When did Mr. 'X' finally die?" In surprise the relative cried out, "Die? He didn't die! He is more alive than ever!" This businessman had proved that evil can continue in your world only if you give your consent to it.

HOW DENIAL HAS HELPED OTHERS

After a recent lecture on the "no" power of healing, most of the people in the audience mentioned to me healings they had witnessed when someone had said "no" to diseased conditions.

A businessman cleared up an asthmatic condition that had plagued him for forty years, as he began denying those asthmatic attacks with "no, no, no."

A nurse, who has often used the "no" power of healing to aid her patients, has also witnessed its results
among members of her family. A brother had been
seriously hurt in an accident. First reports claimed that
a delicate operation would be necessary; and even
then, the outcome was uncertain. To this report, the
nurse kept saying, "No, no, no." After praying for
guidance and getting a feeling of peace about his condition, she assured the family that her brother would
be all right. Further X-rays revealed she was right. No
operation was ever made, and her brother recovered.

A retired engineer attended a religious meeting. In
the midst of it, a lovely lady sitting near him burst into
tears. This man began silently praying, "NO, NO, NO.
THIS IS NOT TRUE. THERE IS NO UNHAPPINESS IN GOD.
THERE NEED BE NO UNHAPPINESS IN ANY OF HIS CREA-
TURES." Suddenly the lady wiped away her tears. The
grief was gone. After the meeting, this man made a
point of introducing himself, so that he might tell the
lady he had prayed for her. She replied, "So that was
it! I knew something had happened, because suddenly
all sorrow left me."

A salesman heard that some former business associates were coming to town from out of state in an effort
to cause trouble for him in his new job. A friend
learned of their scheme late one night and telephoned
this man. The troublesome people were due to arrive
within two days.

Both the friend telephoning and the man involved
knew of the dissolving power of denial. They agreed to
say "no" to this plot. The denial they used was this:
"THERE IS NOTHING TO FEAR, FOR THERE IS NO POWER TO
HURT OR BE HURT IN THIS SITUATION." Both privately
filled their minds with this thought for a long time that
night, and for the next two days.

Their mental action brought results. No hurt was ever done in the matter. The people planning it "changed their minds" and did not come to town, then or later.

A housewife kept hearing gossip about a neighboring couple's marital difficulties. "NO, NO, NO. IT IS NOT TRUE. I REFUSE TO BELIEVE THIS REPORT. IT IS A LIE AND THERE IS NO TRUTH IN IT," this housewife would say to herself in the midst of the gossip.

Soon friends were commenting, "It is amazing. We cannot understand what has happened. All is well with this couple again. The change has come so quickly that it seems a miracle."

HEALED OF CANCER

Several years ago, a nurse told me the story of a radio announcer in her hometown, who was supposed to die of cancer. But his wife knew of the healing power of denial, and she dared to say "no" to the incurable diagnosis.

When his physicians tried to prepare her for the inevitable, she said, "Tell me no more. I refuse to accept that diagnosis. My husband is too fine a man to die. He still has much to give the world."

When no more could be done for him medically, he was sent home from the hospital, presumably to die. But, instead, he lived. As he met regularly with a neighborhood prayer group, the improvement in his health began immediately. Within a few months he had recovered completely and went back to work.

After his healing, a famous television personality, who had just come through a cancer operation, wrote this radio announcer, asking his secret. "In the first place, don't believe anything anybody tells you about your health, unless they tell that you are going to get well. If they try to tell you anything else, refuse to listen, and refuse to believe anything else. Then ask God what it is He really wants you to do in life. Do not waste a minute. Get busy doing it." Both the television personality and the radio announcer overcame the incurable cancer diagnosis.

THE HEALING POWER OF SILENCE

If you will stop nourishing the thought of evil in your life, it will starve for lack of attention and fade away. To every suggestion of evil boldly assert: "There is no evil." To all talk of evil about you — scandals, descriptions of disease, accounts of death and disasters, dangers, financial and family problems — say, "THIS IS NOT TRUE. THERE IS NO EVIL. ONLY GOOD SHALL COME FROM THIS." Many problems have been healed by that thought alone.

Since good is omnipresent, it is even in the midst of evil appearances. *Nothing is evil that brings forth good*, and something good can come from every experience, if only one person will have the courage to dare to look for that good. Realizing this, Emerson wrote: "Every evil to which we do not succumb is a benefactor."

Do not feel obliged to join in conversations that dwell upon the dark side of life. Silence is better than assent to evil appearances. Silence is not only a virtue but one of the greatest denials of all.

Another housewife was told in secret by her husband's physician that he had cancer and could not live more than six months. This wise woman, knowing the law of denial, did not divulge this diagnosis to anyone. Instead of telling her husband he was going home to die, she insisted that his operation had been a success, and he would be all right. He believed her. She also told relatives, neighbors, friends the same thing. Instead of living only six months, this man lived a healthy life for ten more years. When he did die, it was from a sudden bout with pneumonia.

One of the finest ways you can invoke the healing law of denial is in just keeping quiet about your problems, as did this woman. Stop feeding them the substance of your thoughts, words, and emotions. Also watch that you do not criticize in secret; that you cease from even silently finding fault with another. Put away sarcasm from your speech. Stop complaining. Do not prophesy evil for yourself or another. The ancient Greeks avoided a grumbler or one who foretold misfortune, believing he brought them bad luck. Refrain from accusing others of evil in any form.

Cease from petty statements about yourself or others. For instance, do not call your children "bad." Stop referring to the faults of your family, business associates, neighbors, friends. Have a good word for yourself and others, or keep quiet. Silence is your denial of apparent evil.

There is no healing power available to anyone who describes hurts and pains. There is no healing power found in describing evil. Evil can exist only so long as you give it your consent. Only man's belief in evil makes him subject to it!

NOTHING NEW ABOUT DENIAL

There is nothing new about the power of denial to free man from his problems. All religions have recognized that the denial of evil is a constitutional part of faith. The acts of sacrifice, fasting, penitence were all forms of denial with the ancient Hebrews. Both the Hebrews and the ancient Greeks looked to their priests to bring their sins to light and erase (deny) them; they felt that when this was done, their diseases would be healed. The Hebrew word for "evil" was "aven" which meant "nothing." They knew that evil was nothing; that it had no power.

One of the early Christians, Anthanasius, known as the "father of Orthodoxy," said in 373 A.D.: "For evils must be called non-existent, for Good is really existent, as having God for its true author."

St. Augustine said, "There is no evil." Socrates said that men act wrongly because they think wrongly. Plato found that evil is only a way of believing, and is not omnipotent. Emerson delivered an address before the senior class of Divinity College, Cambridge in 1838 in which he explained: "God is positive. Evil is merely privative, not absolute. Evil is like cold, which is the privation of heat. All evil is so much non-reality."

These great men knew that by saying "no" to evil beliefs and appearances in your life, you first dissolve any fear you have had about them. You next dissolve their power to affect you in any way. With the dissolution of the fear comes dissolution of the problem, which falls apart. It had no power except that generated by your previous fear and negative belief in it.

If people the world over invoked the healing power of denial, they could quickly revolutionize their health, and their lives!

The Bible points out the healing law of denial. The prophet Hosea advised: "Take with you words and return unto Jehovah; say unto Him, Take away all iniquity (denial), and accept that which is good (affirmation)." (Hosea 14:2)

Jesus pointed out in the Sermon on the Mount: "Let your speech be yea, yea (affirmation) and nay, nay (denial)." (Matthew 5:37) He referred to the healing power of denial when he spoke of cleansing the inside of the cup, and when he advised: "Judge not according to appearance, but judge righteous judgment." (John 7:24)

Since the dawn of civilization, people have used the sign of the cross as a form of denial. It is a symbol of crossing out man's troubles and sorrows. The up-and-down stroke of the cross means that "nothing has evil power." The right-and-left stroke of the cross means that "the good now reigns." Even primitive man knew through his worship of the cross, that he must cross out the belief in evil, if he wanted life's blessings.

When Jesus said to take up the cross and follow Him (Matthew 16:24), He meant to take up your power of erasure, your power of crossing out limited ideas from your thinking, and use it; that only as you did, could you follow Him into resurrected good.

Long before the time of Jesus, the ancient philosophers substained this belief with the saying: "No cross, no crown."

HOW TO MAKE YOUR CROSS A CROWN

You can begin now to make your cross a crown as you daily use some of the following famous denials, most of which have been used by mankind down through the ages, in one form or another to meet a particular need or situation:

1. THERE IS NO EVIL. NOTHING IS EVIL WHICH BRINGS FORTH GOOD, AND ONLY GOOD SHALL COME FROM THIS.

2. THERE IS NOTHING TO FEAR. THERE IS NO POWER TO HURT. ANYTHING IN MY LIFE THAT NEEDS TO BE CHANGED CAN BE CHANGED!

3. NO, NO, NO. IT IS NOT SO. I DO NOT ACCEPT THIS APPEARANCE. GOD'S EVERLASTING GOOD NOW REIGNS SUPREME AND QUICKLY APPEARS.

4. MY LIFE (MY HEALTH, MY PROSPERITY, MY HAPPINESS, MY SUCCESS, MY GOOD) CANNOT BE LIMITED! I AM UNFETTERED AND UNBOUND.

5. THERE IS NO ABSENCE OF LIFE, SUBSTANCE OR INTELLIGENCE ANYWHERE, SO THERE IS NO ABSENCE OF LIFE, SUBSTANCE OR INTELLIGENCE HERE AND NOW.

6. THERE IS NO PERSONALITY SUCH AS THIS IN THE UNIVERSE. THERE IS NOTHING BUT GOD'S GOOD. I AM IN TRUE RELATIONSHIP WITH ALL PEOPLE AND ALL SITUATIONS NOW.

7. THERE IS NO LOSS, LACK, DISAPPOINTMENT, SICKNESS, PAIN OR DEATH ON MY PATHWAY. THERE IS NOTHING BUT GOD'S ABUNDANT GOOD.

8. THERE IS NOTHING TO FEAR, FOR GREATER IS HE THAT IS WITHIN ME THAN HE THAT IS WITHIN THE WORLD.

9. THERE IS NOTHING TO OPPOSE MY GOOD. THERE IS NO ONE TO OPPOSE MY GOOD. ALL OBSTACLES AND BARRIERS TO THE SUPREMACY OF SPIRIT ARE NOW DISSOLVED, IN THE NAME OF JESUS CHRIST.

THE "SURPRISE" LAW
OF HEALING

— Chapter 3 —

A leading doctor has stated that more progress was made in medical science in the last twenty-five years than in the last twenty-five centuries. He predicted that within two more generations the average length of life, now seventy, will be doubled; and that there will no longer be incurable diseases.

While engineers, nuclear physicists, and other research scientists work with the medical profession to help make these predictions come true, there is something *you* can do to help.

You can invoke the *surprise law* of healing.

Though Jesus pointed it out twenty centuries ago (Luke 5:20-26), the surprise law of healing is still a surprise to most people. It is the law of forgiveness.

It is an immutable mental and spiritual law that when there is a health problem, there is a forgiveness

43

problem. You must forgive if you want to be permanently healed. When you by-pass forgiveness, you by-pass permanent health.

The surprise is in how many people try to find their way back to health without first cleansing their emotions of the cause of their diseases. Health cannot be accepted by a body that is filled with the poisons generated by unforgiveness. Ancient philosophers had a basic statement they used for healing: "THERE IS NOTHING TO HATE."

SECRET HATE MAY CAUSE CANCER

A puzzled lady said to a friend, "I cannot understand it. I have the nicest neighbor who is dying of cancer. It seems so unfair, because this is one of the kindest, gentlest people I know."

The friend replied, "She may seem kind and gentle, but if she is dying of cancer, then there is some old negative emotion that is literally consuming the cells of her body. There is probably someone she hates."

When the puzzled visitor replied, "No, that cannot be," she was advised: "Search further and you will find there is something or someone this person needs to forgive. Always where there is a health problem, there is a forgiveness problem."

Later the mystery was cleared up. The one in doubt reported: "You were right. I learned quite by accident that this neighbor has a relative whom she violently hates. They have not spoken in thirty years."

The nature of cancer may indicate some secret resentment or bitterness. Though one has been outwardly sweet and submissive, he has been inwardly grieved, hurt, intolerant, and severely critical. As in all forms of disease, unwise living habits are usually indicated, too. That is the blessing of learning how to think right. As one employs proper thinking, he unconsciously relates it to proper rest, diet, exercise, and other health habits.

NEGATIVE EMOTIONS FASTEN DISEASE TO YOU

The act of forgiveness dissolves the negative attitudes and memories that are lodged in the conscious and subconscious levels of your mind. Since your mind is located right within your body, your thoughts and emotions occupy space in the cells, bloodstream, and organs of your physical being. Unless a mental and emotional cleansing takes place, such negative emotions fasten your health problems to you.

In spite of advances in scientific and medical research, no pill has yet been created that can cause a sick person to do the first thing he should do, metaphysically, toward gaining permanent health — forgive.

NOTHING UNPLEASANT ABOUT FORGIVENESS

Among the greatest healers of all times were the Kahunas of Hawaii, who through the use of mind power, clairvoyance and secret techniques developed over the centuries, knew how to perform such feats as fire walking, looking into and changing the future, controlling the weather, performing instantaneous healings, curing the mentally obsessed, and raising the dead.

Max Freedom Long spent many years learning their secrets, which he reveals in his fascinating book, *The Secret Science Behind Miracles*.[1] He discovered they knew healing principles, some of which are now advocated by modern psychology. For instance, the Kahunas knew that cleansing the mind of guilt complexes (which they described as "something eating inside") was one of the first laws of healing. To achieve this they conducted a "forgiveness ceremony," which proved a powerful ritual for healing.

There is nothing unpleasant or embarrassing about the act of forgiveness. Your "forgiveness ceremony" can be very simple. To forgive does not mean that you have to bow and scrape to those whom you feel have offended you. To forgive means to "give for," to "replace" the ill feeling, to gain a sense of peace and harmony again. To forgive literally means to "give up" that which you should not have held to in the first place!

In most instances, you need make no outer contact with those involved in your forgiveness act, unless an occasion arises that demands it. If such an occasion does arise, it will be a part of the healing process. As you change your attitudes toward others, they will unconsciously respond by changing their attitudes toward you.

A businessman began to practice daily forgiveness. He had been out of harmony with a number of business associates. It was affecting his health and his prosperity. As he began speaking words of forgiveness, an interesting thing happened:

Business associates with whom he had been at odds appeared everywhere. They made a point of greeting

---

1. Published by DeVorss & Company (Marina del Rey, CA).

him cordially, even when they had to cross a busy street to do so! They treated him more like an old friend than an old enemy. Realizing they had unconsciously forgiven him, his health and his business affairs immediately improved.

HOW TO FORGIVE

There is a simple way you can practice forgiveness. Daily meditate upon and speak forth these words: "ALL THAT HAS OFFENDED ME, I FORGIVE. WHATEVER HAS MADE ME BITTER, RESENTFUL, UNHAPPY, I FORGIVE. WITHIN AND WITHOUT, I FORGIVE. THINGS PAST, THINGS PRESENT, THINGS FUTURE, I FORGIVE."

Sometimes you have to persist. Your first act of forgiveness may not bring the changed attitude and peace that you seek, though it will bring improvement. You did not build up those resentments with one strong negative thought. Neither will one strong positive thought sweep them all away.

A frustrated, overweight, divorced schoolteacher learned of the healing law of forgiveness and surmised that this would be the remedy to her many problems. She vowed to forgive. A week later she jubilantly told a friend, "I have forgiven everybody I know!" But several weeks after that, when the healing power of forgiveness was working deep within her emotions, she reported glumly, "I didn't know I hated so many people."

In an effort to resolve a health problem, a housewife spoke words of forgiveness daily for many weeks. One night just before retiring, her forgiveness prayer was this: "I FORGIVE EVERYTHING AND EVERYBODY WHO CAN POSSIBLY NEED FORGIVENESS IN MY PAST AND PRESENT. I FORGIVE POSITIVELY EVERYONE. I AM FREE AND THEY

ARE FREE, TOO. ALL THINGS ARE CLEARED UP BETWEEN US NOW AND FOREVER."

That night she had a dream in which she remembered a strong feeling of hate she had held toward a relative twenty years previously. That strong emotion welled up in her dream and she cried out, "It is not true. I do not hate you. I forgive you." While speaking those words, she awakened and realized an act of forgiveness had taken place. Though she had not consciously been aware of or even remembered that old hate, when she persisted in speaking words of forgiveness, they had invaded the subconscious levels of her memory and brought it up to be healed.

You may not consciously be aware of what or whom you need to forgive in the past or present. It is not necessary that you know, though often it will be revealed to you, as you invoke forgiveness. The only requirement is that you willingly speak words of forgiveness, and let those words do their cleansing work.

HOW FORGIVENESS BRINGS HEALTH AND WEALTH TO A HOUSEWIFE

Genuine forgiveness is not a casual act. The word means a "cleansing," "a blotting out of transgression." Forgiveness is wrought in the very texture of the soul. It takes time and persistence for true forgiveness to invade the subconscious levels.

A housewife learned of the healing law of forgiveness, and began to use it, hoping for improvement of her health. For an entire year she daily decreed: "I FULLY AND FREELY FORGIVE. I LOOSE AND LET GO. I LET GO AND LET GOD DO HIS PERFECT WORK OF HEALING IN MY MIND, BODY, AND AFFAIRS."

When a long-standing health problem faded away, her doctor said it was a miracle. She said it was the miracle of forgiveness. At the end of that year, she also received another miracle—a large inheritance—from one of the people she had just spent a year forgiving!

A MILLIONAIRE'S HEALTH SECRET

Resentment, condemnation, anger, the desire to "get even" or to see someone punished or hurt, are things that rot your soul and tear down your health. You must forgive injuries and hurts of the past and present, not so much for the other person's sake, as for your own.

A retired businessman, past seventy, related the secret of his amazing vitality, business success, and personal happiness, which included a lovely youthful bride:

"Several times a week I play golf with some old business cronies, who are retired. We play only for friendship's sake. They are no competition on the golf course because during the last ten years they have 'fallen apart.' The reason they are in ill health and old beyond their age is this: They spend all their time looking back, talking about the business problems they had years ago, and about all the people who wronged them. They constantly criticize and find fault. Their unforgiving attitudes have wrecked their health—and their golf game.

"I discovered long ago that I must constantly forgive if I want to be healthy and happy. Forgiving is easier than most folks think, especially when you make a habit of it. And it's worth the effort. All that I have now in the way of health, wealth and happiness has come from forgiving and forgetting the hurts of the past."

FORGIVENESS DISSOLVES LUMP

Hurt or hate of any kind scars the soul and works an illness in the flesh. The illness will not be fully healed while you continue to remain unforgiving.

A woman discovered a lump in her breast. Instead of frantically rushing out to negatively discuss it with others, she decided to analyze the situation mentally and pray for guidance.

She realized that a hard condition in the body indicates a corresponding hard condition in the mind. She prayed, "Father, what hard thoughts of resentment, condemnation or unforgiveness am I holding? What or whom do I need to forgive?"

Since the answer did not come immediately, she continued every day to pray, meditate, and ask: "What hard attitudes do I need to release and give up, in order to be forgiven this condition? In meditation one day she found herself thinking about her husband and a woman with whom he had been involved five years previously. At the time, she had met the experience nonresistantly, and it had faded away. She and her husband were now happier than ever, but she realized in this meditation period that she still held hard thoughts about that distressing period.

For the "other woman" she decreed: "I FREELY FORGIVE YOU. I LOOSE YOU AND LET YOU GO. IT IS DONE. IT IS FINISHED FOREVER."

To her husband she mentally said: "I FREELY FORGIVE YOU. I LET GO ALL FALSE CONCEPTS ABOUT YOU. YOU

ARE A FAITHFUL, LOVING HUSBAND, AND WE HAVE A WON-
DERFUL MARRIAGE. ONLY GOOD HAS COME FROM THAT
EXPERIENCE."

She declared those words of forgiveness in her daily
prayer time for several weeks. One day she realized
that the lump in her breast was gone; she never knew
when it disappeared.

THE BINDING POWER OF HATE

When you hold resentment toward another, you are
bound to that person or condition by an emotional link
that is stronger than steel. Forgiveness is the only way
to dissolve that link and get free.

A nurse was seriously injured in a collision with a car
operated by a drunken driver. After recovering from
the accident she returned to her nursing profession.
Again and again the man responsible for the collision
was admitted to the hospital where she worked, always
in an intoxicated condition.

Being resentful of the trouble he had caused her, she
refused to nurse him, and was assured by his doctor
that she would not be assigned to his case.

One night there was a shortage of help on her floor,
and she was the only nurse available when the light
came on from this patient's room. Since it was unavoid-
able she delivered his tray and medicine. When she appeared, he recognized her, talked about the accident,
and told her he had been worried about her financial
affairs, realizing that she was widowed with children to
feed.

As they talked, he asked forgiveness and she gave it.
Peace came. The amazing thing was that soon after

their conversation, he was released from the hospital, and she never heard of his being admitted there again. This man had wanted forgiveness from the one he had hurt. When he got it, he faded out of her life.

HOW HATE ATTRACTS

A businesswoman proved the attracting power of hate.

Her lover had died. Though he had conducted a love affair with her for more than a decade, at death he was still married to a faithful wife. His sudden death left his former mistress filled with hate for his wife, who inherited his fortune.

As this businesswoman's hate grew, so did her problems. She began plying her system with drink and drugs. Though in a highly nervous state, she was forced to return to work in an effort to meet her mounting debts, and took a job as a store clerk. Ironically, her former lover's widow began shopping in this store and seemed drawn to this woman's department. The widow had known nothing of this woman's connection with her late husband, and did not realize what she was asking emotionally, when she would approach this sales lady for advice about certain items.

Frantically this saleswoman asked, "Why is this happening to me? Haven't I been through enough?" Then she realized the irony of hate and its fantastic attracting power.

After she began daily speaking words of forgiveness for the entire situation, the rich widow faded out of her life. As this saleswoman gradually cleansed her mind of hate, she was able to resume a normal life and later happily married.

A FORGIVENESS FORMULA

It is easier to forgive those you are inclined to condemn, resent, even hate, when you remember this:

They have not really failed nor disappointed you. They have not even let you down. They may have stumbled while crossing your pathway. But, in reality, they are sons of God who temporarily lost their way.

If they crossed your pathway, it was because they needed and wanted your blessing. They were unconsciously looking to you to be steadied and set right. Your progress has not been hindered, no matter what they did. They cannot keep your good from you.

They crossed your pathway by divine appointment, even though they seemed to hurt you for awhile. *When people bother you in any way, it is because their souls are trying to get your divine attention and your blessing.* Give them that,[2] and they will no longer bother you, as they fade out of your life and find their good elsewhere. Meanwhile, divine restoration will occur in your own affairs.

A nurse proved the truth of these ideas. She was married to a man who had been previously married. Upon learning of his second marriage, his former wife spread ugly rumors. One day this former wife got very sick and was admitted to the hospital where the nurse (the second wife) worked. This nurse was informed by her superior: "Your husband's former wife is here as a patient. You do not have to attend her."

The nurse replied, "I would rather not, but if it works out that way, I will not refuse."

---

2. The method for blessing others is described in Chapter 2 of the author's book, *The Prosperity Secrets of the Ages.*

One day it did work out that way. When the nurse answered a call and saw the agony her husband's former wife was going through, she realized what a high price this woman was paying for her previous words of criticism. "Lord, have mercy on her, for she knows not what she has done," was the nurse's prayer of forgiveness for this patient.

When this patient recovered, she never gossiped about the nurse again.

Forgiveness begins with the one who recognizes the offense. When you get the offense out of your own heart, you have forgiven. The reconciliation which you bring about within yourself will have its effect upon your brother, and there will be an automatic forgiving on his part toward you, either consciously or unconsciously.

WHEN YOUR GOOD IS DELAYED

Often people try to shrug off the need for forgiveness: "That is not my problem. I have nothing to forgive."

If you have a problem, you have something to forgive. Anyone who experiences pain has a need to forgive. Anyone who finds himself in unpleasant circumstances has a need to forgive. Anyone who finds himself in debt has a need to forgive. Where there is suffering, unhappiness, lack, confusion or misery of any sort, there is a need to forgive.

There is an old proverb: "He who cannot forgive others breaks the bridge over which he himself must pass one day."

When your good is delayed, that is the time to forgive. Often everything stands still, and there is a deadlock, until forgiveness is released into the situation *by you.*

A young couple had long sought to adopt a child. They were a healthy, happy, prosperous, intelligent couple; yet adoption agencies constantly turned them down. It was a baffling problem.

One day the wife learned that when your good is delayed, it indicates a need for forgiveness. As she began to daily practice forgiveness, decreeing: "I FULLY AND FREELY FORGIVE ANYONE OR ANYTHING THAT NEEDS FORGIVENESS IN MY PAST OR PRESENT," old hurts, resentments, grudges, prejudices and unhappy memories came to her attention. To each she said, "I FORGIVE YOU AND RELEASE YOU." A sense of peace was established.

Later she learned of an out-of-town adoption agency with which she had had no previous communication. Contact with them led to the adoption of a lovely baby. *Forgiveness can sweep aside all that has delayed you in your race toward good.* This adopting mother proved it.

WHEN THE SAME PROBLEM RE-OCCURS

Often the same problem presents itself to you again and again, in various guises, until it is released through forgiveness.

Another housewife had a baffling problem: An early marriage had ended with the death of her young husband. During a second marriage that followed, she

soon realized that she was facing the same set of problems she had faced in her first marriage, though she was
now living hundreds of miles away, amid a new set of
circumstances and amid new people.

Her main problem was with her mother-in-law who
would not accept her, who kept interfering, in an attempt to dominate her husband.

One day as this wife prayed, "Father, what is the
truth about this situation?" the thought flashed to her:
"You had trouble with your first mother-in-law. She,
too, tried to alienate your husband from you. You
never forgave her. Here is the same problem again."

Relieved to have the answer, this young wife began
daily calling the name of that first mother-in-law,
mentally saying to her; "I FULLY AND FREELY FORGIVE
YOU. I LOOSE YOU AND LET YOU GO. ALL ILL FEELING HAS
BEEN CLEARED UP BETWEEN US NOW AND FOREVER." She
also used this same treatment on her present mother-
in-law.

This proved to be the answer in producing emotional release and relief. Harmony and freedom from
interference resulted.

A doctor of divinity once said that if Jesus had not
dared to say on the cross, "Father, forgive them for
they know not what they do," He could not have experienced resurrection. (Luke 23:34)

*If only one person will dare to forgive, the problem
can be solved, regardless of who else is involved, and
whether anyone else wants to forgive.*

The person who dares to forgive gains control of the
situation. He may not have appeared to have had any
prior power to solve the problem. But suddenly there
will be a change. The situation will begin to shift and
rearrange itself. The person who forgives will find a

divine solution appearing. *The forgiving state of mind is a magnetic power for attracting good. No good thing can be withheld from the forgiving state of mind.*

A SURE REMEDY

Along with forgiving others, it is also necessary to forgive yourself. Self-condemnation leads to dire results in matters of health and finances. Sometimes we are unforgiving of circumstances: an unhappy childhood, the loss of or neglect by parents, the loss of some material blessing. Sometimes we are unforgiving of God, blaming our losses, ill health and other problems on Him, instead of realizing they have been self-inflicted.

Charles Fillmore, that Kansas City businessman who co-founded the Unity movement, while experiencing a dramatic healing, once gave a forgiveness formula that has inspired millions. He described it as *A Sure Remedy*:[3]

Here is a mental treatment that is guaranteed to cure every ill, flesh is heir to: Sit for half an hour every night and mentally forgive everyone against whom you have any ill will or antipathy. If you fear or if you are prejudiced against even an animal, mentally ask forgiveness of it and send it thoughts of love. If you have accused anyone of injustice, if you have discussed anyone unkindly, if you have criticized or gossiped about anyone, withdraw your words by asking him, in the silence, to forgive you. If you have had a falling

3. Available in pamphlet form from Unity School of Christianity, Unity Village, MO 64065.

out with friends or relatives, if you are at law, or engaged in contention with anyone, do everything in your power to end the separation. See all things and all persons as they really are—pure Spirit—and send them your strongest thoughts of love. Do not go to bed any night feeling that you have any enemy in the world.

An all-inclusive prayer of forgiveness is this: "I FOR- GIVE EVERYTHING, EVERYONE, EVERY EXPERIENCE, EVERY MEMORY OF THE PAST OR PRESENT THAT NEEDS FORGIVE- NESS. I FORGIVE POSITIVELY EVERYONE. GOD IS LOVE, AND I AM FORGIVEN AND GOVERNED BY GOD'S LOVE ALONE. GOD'S LOVE IS NOW ADJUSTING MY LIFE AND ITS PROBLEMS. REALIZING THIS, I ABIDE IN PEACE."

HOW TO INVOKE FORGIVENESS FROM OTHERS

As previously stated, you have the power to deliber- ately speak words that will cause others to forgive you.

A housewife had large painful lumps under both arms. She feared a medical examination, realizing it would probably produce an incurable diagnosis and a major operation. Her prayers for healing had seemed unavailing, though, until she learned of the healing law of forgiveness. Even then, as she spoke prayers of forgiveness toward others, nothing dramatic occurred in her health. But when she began to speak words of forgiveness for others *toward* her, something dramatic did occur. The lumps under her arms, with their atten- dant swelling and pain, began to subside, and finally disappeared.

FORGIVE BY GIVING UP

Along with speaking words to produce forgiveness, sometimes it is necessary to do something dramatic in an outer way to produce satisfactory results. The word "forgive" means "to give up." At times the greatest way to forgive others, and to get them to forgive you, is to give them up.

Through divorce a businesswoman had been deprived of the love and companionship of her son for more than a decade. Even though she had remarried happily and well, she had bitterly held on to the unhappy divorce memories of the past, and a sense of the loss of her child.

Then suddenly she heard from her son again, and made plans for a long-awaited reunion. But when it occurred it was a bitter disappointment. Her son not only seemed like a stranger to her, but he proceeded to deliberately praise her ex-husband over and over— even though it was this ex-husband who had kept them apart for so long. Furthermore, her son seemed uninterested in their reunion, past the point of its monetary possibilities for him and his future. After his unsatisfactory visit, he returned home, quit his job, and continually demanded money from his mother.

She happily complied, until she learned that most of the money she sent her son was going to her ex-husband, and that her son had lost all incentive either to work or to get an education.

Meanwhile, as she had tried to effect what turned out to be a one-sided reconciliation, a number of old health problems hit her with renewed force. Gradually she realized that old animosities had been stirred up within her, which might be affecting her health. And since her better-than-average lifestyle had been a surprise to her son and ex-husband, she may have unconsciously absorbed their resentments toward her.

She decided to forgive them by giving up all further contact with them. She explained to her son that if and when his motives were for sincere reconciliation, and not for mere monetary gain, perhaps their relationship could be re-established. His lack of gratitude for the help she had so generously extended, and his lack of a reply, freed her from any further false sense of responsibility. Her freedom from this relationship also freed her from the health problems it had apparently caused.

When she "forgave" by "giving up," her health problems gave her up as well!

A DYNAMIC STATEMENT FOR FORGIVENESS

A fine statement to use for the forgiveness of others toward you, is this:

"I AM NOW FORGIVEN BY EVERYTHING AND EVERYONE OF THE PAST AND PRESENT THAT NEEDS TO FORGIVE ME. I AM NOW POSITIVELY FORGIVEN BY EVERYONE."

You can be assured that:

Forgiveness is all powerful. Forgiveness heals all ills. Forgiveness makes the weak strong. Forgiveness makes the cowardly courageous. Forgiveness makes the ignorant wise. Forgiveness makes the mournful happy. *Forgiveness can unblock whatever has stood between you and your good. Let it.*

THE HEALING LAW
OF RELEASE

— Chapter 4 —

It may come as a surprise to you that the emotional cause of your health problems can be possessiveness and strong attachment to (or by) some person, situation or condition in your life. It may come as a further surprise that you must emotionally release (or gain release from) that person, situation or condition in order to bring healing into your own mind, body, and affairs.

Your affections strongly affect your health. Back of every disease is a misdirection of the affectional nature. Any disturbance of the affections unbalances one's health.

Although we have often thought of intense emotional attachment as one of the highest forms of love, quite the opposite is true: When that intense emotional attachment takes the form of possessiveness, it leads to bondage; whereas the way of true love is to free that which we love, in the knowledge that the way then opens for a more satisfying type of love to develop. *One never loses anything worth having through release. Release is magnetic and draws to you your own.*

If through strong emotional ties, you direct the substance of your thoughts and feelings into someone else's life, which you should be using in your own, the lack then appears as ill health or some other form of imbalance in your own life.

The word "release" means a "setting free," a "liberation." *Often it is not an enemy you need to release emotionally, but a relative or friend. A fine healing formula is to forgive your enemies and release your friends!*

Kahlil Gibran has advised in *The Prophet*:

> Love one another but make not a bond of love. Let there be spaces in your togetherness . . . Stand together, yet not too near together.[1]

We often try to bend others to our will, calling it love, when it is only selfish possessiveness. Then we wonder why those involved do not appreciate our "help" and why they react negatively.

---

1. Reprinted from *The Prophet* by Kahlil Gibran, with permission of the publisher, Alfred A. Knopf, Inc., New York. Copyright 1923 by Kahlil Gibran; renewal copyright 1951 by Administrators S.T.A. of Kahlil Gibran estate, and Mary G. Gibran.

HOW THEY HEALED THEIR SPOUSES

A housewife had worried for months over her husband's illness. The more she tried to help him recover, the more he clung to his illness. One day she learned of the healing law of release and said secretly to her husband: "I LOVE YOU, BUT I RELEASE YOU TO COMPLETE FREEDOM AND COMPLETE HEALTH IN WHATEVER WAY IS BEST."

When this wife had previously tried to help her husband by using various healing affirmations, he subconsciously resisted her attempts to will him back to health. When she released him to find health in his own way, ceasing any mental effort in his direction, his former ailments disappeared.

In the area of health, the power of release is all important. A woman with a severe cold coughed all night. Not able to sleep, her husband arose before dawn, and invoked the healing law of release for her, as he said silently: "You may cough all you like. I release your cough. It is nothing at all." Quickly his wife relaxed into a deep sleep. Upon awakening she was completely refreshed. The cough was gone.

THE TRANSFORMING POWER OF RELEASE

A young minister had been suffering severe abdominal pains for several days, though his physician could find nothing physically wrong. The prescribed medicine had not eased the pain, and this young man was anxious to recover, so that he might leave the next day for a ministers' conference in a distant state.

He finally related his predicament to a friend who realized there must be an emotional cause for the pain. Conversation revealed that this young minister was upset because he had been relieved of his church duties and was scheduled for transfer to another type of work by his denomination. Though he had mentioned his feelings to no one, he secretly felt an injustice had been done.

Together these two friends decreed: "I FULLY AND FREELY RELEASE THIS JOB TRANSFER. I LOOSE IT AND LET IT GO. I LET GO AND LET GOD'S PERFECT GOOD MANIFEST THROUGH ALL THESE CHANGES. ONLY GOOD SHALL COME FROM THIS."

By the next morning, all pain was gone and he departed for that ministers' conference.

At the conference, it was announced that some scholarships were available to ministers who wished to do graduate study in a specialized field of religion. This young man applied and was granted a scholarship. Instead of having to take the job to which he had been apparently unfairly transferred, he left the state to study at a well-known seminary. There he met his future wife. Later he became a professor of religion and settled down to a happy life. By speaking words of release, this young minister had set into operation a series of events that led to much more than just a physical healing! This often happens.

HEALED OF LEUKEMIA THROUGH RELEASE

In the case of more serious diagnoses, the healing power of release can prove equally effective.

In 1949 a woman was "blessed with leukemia" —

these are her words. She feels that the experience was a blessing because it caused her to seek God and prove His goodness. Through this healing she learned of the omnipotent power of release.

After the diagnosis of "incurable" was passed on her case, she remembered that a friend had been healed of cancer of the brain through faith and prayer. Memory of that supposed incurable healing gave this woman the courage to believe she, too, could be healed.

As she prayed, "Thy will be done, Father. You healed her and You can heal me," all fear of death left her. However, the pain, swelling and other unhealthy symptoms continued.

One night when she had been given up to die, she weakly released herself into God's keeping: "Father, nobody on this earth is going to try to do anything for me. It is all up to You now. I release, loose, let go, and let Thy good will be done."

She drifted off into a restful sleep after whispering this prayer. When she awakened the next morning, all swelling was gone from her body. Seventeen pounds had disappeared overnight! She felt so good that she asked for her favorite food, and wanted no more liquid diets.

Even though for months she had not gotten out of bed, she soon was walking blocks each day, up hill and down, rejoicing and giving thanks that she had been healed. Her neighbors thought they were seeing a ghost. When her physician examined her and found every part of her body perfect, he commented that she had certainly "worked the Lord overtime."

Further proof of her healing came later when she had some teeth extracted. Such oral surgery was supposed to be fatal to anyone with leukemia. Yet, for

her, it was an uneventful experience. Several decades
have passed since this healing; yet this woman has remained in good health.

RELEASE PRODUCES HARMONY
FOR DIVORCEE'S OLD AND NEW FAMILIES

On all levels of life, we need to practice release.
*Often we think we want freedom from our problems,
when in reality, our problems want freedom from us!
Though it can be ego-jolting, when we give them that
freedom, they usually dissolve.*

For ten years a divorcee and her former husband
waged a legal battle over the custody of their children.
And for ten years both experienced ill health, financial
problems and emotional frustration.

Finally, this divorcee learned about the healing
power of release. As she began to release her children
into God's care, she met and happily married a fine
widower. He attempted to help her legally claim her
children, who were living with her former husband.
For some months, a legal squabble ensued. Bitterly she
wrote about the problems she was facing.

It was suggested that she not only release her
children to God's care, but also her former husband,
whom she had continued to condemn. Relieved to
know what to do, she began daily decreeing to him
mentally: "I FULLY AND FREELY RELEASE YOU. I LOOSE
YOU AND LET YOU GO. ALL THAT HAS HAPPENED BETWEEN
US IS RELEASED NOW AND FOREVER. I FREE YOU TO YOUR
HIGHEST GOOD."

This proved to be the miracle prayer. The former
husband, who had remained unmarried for ten years,
soon remarried. The new wife convinced him that if

his former one wanted their children, she should be allowed to have them since she was now emotionally and financially capable of giving them every blessing.

Later the mother of these children wrote: "How powerful is that healing law of release! My children and I are now 'living happily ever after' with my fine new husband on his lovely country estate. What a contrast to those lean years we spent in a crowded apartment, facing all kinds of emotional and financial problems alone."

RELEASE PRODUCES RIGHT JOB

A public relations consultant was having business problems. For some time he had had his own private company. With the help of an assistant, he had represented many fine firms, successfully handling their publicity. Then came a decline in business, which caused him to realize that a change was apparently trying to take place in his career.

He applied for several fine jobs that were available in his part of the country, his personal choice being one in his own town, representing a large medical center. This prestige position would entail interesting travel and personal contact with some of the finest medical authorities in America. Of course, the job would also assure him of financial security.

But as the weeks passed, something delayed the decision about this and several other positions in which he was interested. Those in charged seemed unable to make a decision about who to hire.

As his affairs faltered, he sought the counsel of his minister who said, "There is a block. The block is within you. There is something you need to release. When

you do, the right job will open to you." After quiet con-
templation of this startling news, the businessman replied, "Why, of course! My wife and I have agreed that
a change in jobs would be good. But we are in the process of adopting a child, and one of the requirements is
that we remain residents of this state. We wanted a better job, but we also wanted this child."

His minister replied, "The good of one is the good of
all. If this child is yours by divine right, all legal matters will work out harmoniously in conjunction with
your residence and work. Place the entire situation in
God's hands and release it to the perfect solution. The
pieces will then fall into place." Together they prayed
the prayer of release. At home this man and his wife
also spoke words of release.

Within a few days this executive heard from the
medical center. They stated that he had been appointed as their new public relations consultant. Later
this couple became the proud legal parents of their
adopted child.

*Your problems do not create themselves. You create
them by your own fearful thinking. Through speaking
words of release, those problems are then freed to work
out in whatever way is best.*

THE PROBLEM-SOLVING POWER OF RELEASE
IN CLOSE RELATIONSHIPS

Release is a setting free, a liberation. *When you
want to be set free from ill health and liberated from
other problems, you should speak words of release,
both for yourself and others.*

A strong-willed woman kept saying, "It's too bad my
husband is such a failure in business. *I* am the brains

in this family. If I did not help run our business, we would go broke."

One day she got sick and for three months was unable to go near their place of business. Through illness she was forced to release their business to be run by her husband in whatever way he deemed best.

It was a shock to this woman to learn that she was *not* "the brains of the family"; that her husband was perfectly capable of transacting their business affairs in an entirely successful manner. Later she said, "How grateful I am for that illness. It caused me to release my husband and our business to greater success than I could have dreamed possible."

Your dear ones must have liberty to live their own lives, and you must grant it to them, or else you will create problems for them and for yourself. *If you want to be free from all types of problems in mind, body, and affairs, then emotionally, you must release other people to find their good in their own way. A clear channel is then opened for great good to come to all involved.* Your own freedom and well-being depend upon such release, as does the freedom and well-being of your loved ones.

A professional woman was quite concerned about her bachelor son. He was successful in his work but had never married, and still lived with his mother. A widow, she had devoted many years of her life to rearing and educating this son. She felt the time had come for her to be free to travel and perhaps to enter another field of work. She also longed to see her son happily married, with a home and family of his own. She realized that her own freedom depended upon the emotional release of her son.

Then it seemed that her dreams were coming true. Her son met the girl of his choice. But instead of being

happy about it, his mother became upset and resentful, constantly finding fault with the girl. When she
got sick, her physician stated she was suffering from
hypertension caused by some "secret anxiety."

She wisely surmised that in order to be free from this
illness she must free her son to live his life as he saw fit.
She began daily decreeing: "I FULLY AND FREELY RELEASE
YOU. I LOOSE YOU AND LET YOU GO TO YOUR GOOD. THE
GOOD OF ONE IS THE GOOD OF ALL." The anxiety left her,
the health problem faded away, and her son married.
She was then free for the life she had secretly longed
for.

*When your prayers have not been answered, though
you have conscientiously sought that answer through
spiritual methods, it is usually an indication that you
need to practice release—release of some person or
situation; release of some financial or health problem.
As you do, you open the way for your problems to be
resolved.*

HOW FREEDOM CAN BE THE TURNING POINT TO HAPPINESS, SUCCESS AND HEALING

Most human relations problems would melt away if
the people involved would practice the miracle of release, instead of trying to make other people over to
conform to their will and their way.

People who hold tight reins over their spouses and
children often wonder why prosperity and good health
are personally withheld from them. People who hold
tight reins over their friends wonder often why their
own health is so poor and they are unable to get permanent healing.

Setting others free means setting yourself free! When you feel bound to other people, their attitudes, behavior, way of life, it is because you are (perhaps subconsciously) binding them to you. Then you begin to feel bound, chafing against the very bondage *you* have caused. *Always you personally hold the key to your freedom. You turn the key to that freedom when you release the personality, the problem, or the condition that you think is clutching you.* You are the master, never the slave, of circumstances. *You become victor instead of victim when you dare to speak the word of release to and for the person or thing you think is binding you.*

A peaceful, poised woman was married to a cantankerous, dominating man twenty years her senior. Yet they appeared compatible. When asked how she lived in harmony with her husband's stubborn disposition, this woman quietly replied, "When my husband gets difficult, I just silently release him. He invariably calms down and does the right thing."

Parents of teenagers have found this technique helpful. *People have a way of unconsciously doing the right thing when they are emotionally freed to do so.*

In cases of alcoholism, drug addiction and other forms of mental illness, the use of release has often proved to be the turning point toward recovery.

RELEASE THROUGH DEATH

Often in matters of "life and death," we clutch to us people who want to go on to the next plane of life. When a person lingers between life and death, after having had a full life, you can be sure someone is holding them to this earth plane, and they should be freed to go on to their good elsewhere. To such people, death is healing. It can be a welcome release for which their souls long.[2]

A businessman was concerned about his wife who had been in pain for many months from cancer. He said, "I don't think she can take much more and neither can I. What can I do to help her?"

"Release her to be healed in God's own way," was the reply.

This man then decreed for his wife: "I FULLY AND FREELY RELEASE YOU. I LOOSE YOU AND LET YOU GO. I LET GO AND LET GOD HEAL YOU IN HIS OWN WAY." Within a few days this woman passed on quietly in her sleep.

A schoolteacher was concerned about her mother who had been in a coma for more than a year. This beloved mother had a large family of children, who adored her. The daughter said, "I know my mother wants to go on to the next plane of life to be with my father, whom she loved dearly; she has been unconscious for a year in a private nursing home. Most of her estate has been spent in medical care. But I have a brother who gets upset when the possibility of mother's death is mentioned. He seems to be holding her here."

Words of release were spoken for this mother. Words of release were then spoken for her son: "YOU FULLY AND FREELY RELEASE YOUR MOTHER. YOU LOOSE HER AND LET HER GO. YOU LET GO AND LET GOD HEAL YOUR MOTHER IN WHATEVER WAY IS BEST." Within ten days this woman passed on. Surprisingly, her son seemed relieved over his mother's peaceful transition.

---

2. See sub-section entitled "What to Think About Death", in the author's book, *The Prosperity Secrets of the Ages.*

RELEASE CAN BRING RECOVERY

Often when a person is released to his good, instead of dying, he recovers!

A man of wealth was on his death bed, surrounded by attentive relatives whom he felt were more interested in his wealth than in his health. This man seemed torn between a desire to live and a desire to die.

A business friend dropped by to see him one night when he was very low. The sick man shooed his solicitous relatives out of the room, complaining to his friend, "They don't care anything about me. They are just waiting around to get my money." Then he lapsed into a coma.

The visiting friend sat by this man's bed, as he lay unconscious, and said to him, "You are now released from your relatives, so loose them and let them go. They have no power over you. They cannot take your wealth from you. You are free to stay or go. The choice is up to you." That night proved to be the turning point in this man's condition. He rallied, regained consciousness, later made a complete recovery, and again took control of his financial affairs.

HOW TO GAIN FREEDOM FROM POSSESSIVENESS

Your problems are sometimes caused by the possessiveness and strong emotional attachment that other persons have on your life, either through their positive or negative thinking about you. *Your words of release can cause other people to subconsciously release you.*

A government employee suffering from ill health, had been advised by his doctor to move to a different climate. He applied for a job transfer into such an area where there was an opening. For months his application was considered, but nothing happened.

When he and his wife learned of the healing power of release, they realized that hometown relatives did not wish to give them up. This couple gained their freedom by decreeing to their relatives: "YOU FULLY AND FREELY RELEASE US. YOU LOOSE US AND LET US GO. YOU LET GO AND LET GOD'S GOOD MANIFEST IN THIS SITUATION." Soon their relatives said, "As much as we would like you to remain here near us, you must do what is best for your health. We will do all we can to help you make this change." Within a matter of days the transfer had been approved, and they quickly moved to the new job in the new climate.

RELEASE FROM THE DEAD SOLVES MARITAL AND FINANCIAL PROBLEMS

You can speak words of release and gain freedom even from those who passed to the other side of life. Sometimes it seems necessary to do so, especially when the deceased had strong, domineering personalities.

A young husband was so dominated by his mother that he finally left his wife and went home to "live with mother." His wife bitterly said, "If only my mother-in-law was out of the picture, then my husband would come back to me."

One day her wish came true, when her husband's mother died. But this young wife soon discovered that her husband was even more dominated by his mother after she had gone, as he grieved for her, talked about her incessantly, and kept remembering experiences he had shared with her. He even refused to move out of her house. This was frustrating to his wife, who had expected him to rush home.

Finally this young wife learned of the healing law of release and spoke words of release for both mother and son. To the mother on the next plane she said: "YOU FULLY AND FREELY RELEASE YOUR SON TO THIS EARTH LIFE. YOU LOOSE HIM AND LET HIM GO. YOU LET GO AND LET GOD GUIDE YOU IN YOUR NEW EXPERIENCES." To her husband she said: "YOU FULLY AND FREELY RELEASE YOUR MOTHER. YOU LOOSE AND LET HER GO ON TO HER GOOD ELSEWHERE. YOU LET GO AND LET GOD MANIFEST THE PERFECT ADJUSTMENT."

Gradually this man resumed a normal attitude and a normal life, later returning to his wife.

A beautiful lady had been ruled by her adoring husband until his death. His declining health had exhausted their financial assets, and he left her without funds, heavily in debt. Her only hope of financial recovery was through sale of the lovely home they had happily shared together for many years.

Immediately following her husband's death, she placed their house on the market for sale, but for months nothing happened. Finally an intuitive friend said, "Your late husband loved this house. He probably has not released his strong hold upon it, or upon you, even though he is on the next plane. You can gain release from him through the spoken word."

The widow daily began decreeing to her deceased husband: "YOU FULLY AND FREELY RELEASE ME. YOU NOW RELEASE THIS HOUSE. YOU LOOSE AND LET GO. YOU LET GO THIS EARTH PLANE AND MAKE YOUR PERFECT ADJUSTMENT TO YOUR NEW ENVIRONMENT. YOU ARE FREE NOW AND I AM FREE TOO."

The house was soon sold, and other financial matters
quickly resolved.

NOTHING NEW ABOUT RELEASE

The healing law of release has long been emphasized
and practiced in various ways. You've heard it said
that "confession is good for the soul." It is good for the
body, too! The religious practice of confessional is an
exceptionally fine form of release.

Even much less sacred methods of release have healing power. In *The Autobiography of Mark Twain*,[3] he
speaks of a famous pre-Civil War doctor who healed a
patient by making her angry. "She poured out upon
the doctor her whole insulted mind," and she got well.

Sigmund Freud, the founder of psychoanalysis, often healed his patients by causing them to relive consciously repressed experiences of the past. As the old
experience again came to memory, the patient usually
discharged strong emotion, sometimes in tears, sometimes in resentment, hate, or bitterness. When this
pent-up emotion was released, a kind of mental cathar-
sis took place, and the patient was then restored to
health.

In counseling others, I have often found that once
the person releases pent-up negative emotion, his mind
then clears and is free to see a solution to his problems.

The healing power of release, in connection with old
relationships and experiences, is pointed out by Emerson in his essay, *Compensation*:

---

3. Published by Harper & Row (New York, 1959)

We cannot part with our friends. We cannot let our angels go. We do not see that they only go out that arch-angels may come in.[4]

He points out that such release is a necessary part of the law of growth; that such changes operate a revolution in our lives through which we cast off dead circumstances and worn-out relationships, so that new ones "more friendly to the growth of the character" may appear.

RELEASE IS MAGNETIC

Truly, release is magnetic. You never lose anything that is yours by divine right through the act of release. Instead you make way for your own particular good to appear.

A prominent businessman once shared with me his special formula for release. He carried a card on which was printed the following statements. Daily he read them over, thus giving himself a treatment in release. He attributed much of his success to this formula:

"I LET GO MY TENSE HOLD ON PERSONS, PLACES, EVENTS, THINGS. I LET GO WHAT GOES. I AM NOT AFRAID TO LET GO OF POSSESSIVE ATTITUDES TOWARD MY DEAR ONES OR TO- WARD MY POSSESSIONS, FOR I KNOW WHAT MAN HUMANLY RELEASES HE NEVER LOSES, IF IT IS HIS BY DIVINE RIGHT. IT IS ONLY THAT WHICH MAN TRIES TO TENSELY POSSESS THAT SLIPS THROUGH HIS CLOSED FINGERS AND ESCAPES HIM.

---

4. Ralph Waldo Emerson, *The Writings of Ralph Waldo Emerson* (New York, NY: Random House, 1940).

THAT WHICH I WILLINGLY SURRENDER TO GOD, I NEVER
LOSE. THAT OR SOMETHING BETTER WILL ALWAYS BE GIVEN
ME BY MY LOVING FATHER. DIVINE RELEASE PRODUCES
PERFECT RESULTS OF HEALTH, WEALTH AND HAPPINESS FOR
ME AND THROUGH ME NOW."

A marvelous healing statement of release is this:

"I NOW LET GO EVERYTHING AND EVERYBODY OF THE
PAST OR PRESENT THAT HAS CAUSED DISCOMFORT IN,
THROUGH OR ROUND ABOUT ME. WE ALL GO FREE TO
GREATER WHOLENESS."

THE "YES" LAW
OF HEALING

— Chapter 5 —

When asked what his first deed would be if he were to be made Emperor of China, Confucius replied, "I would re-establish the precise meaning of words."

He knew that words have a dynamic power to kill or to cure, and should be used carefully. All religions, cultures, and civilizations have known and taught that *your word is your power.*

Your words are constantly doing one of two things: building up or tearing down; healing or destroying. Every word you speak goes forth from your mouth charged with atomic energies. Good words are alive with life, health, and vitality.

The universal life current within you is subject to your words. Your every word is recorded in your body, so that your words become your flesh. You literally "eat your words."

Every thought has a power peculiar to itself. Every word, when spoken, vibrates throughout your whole body and moves every cell and atom of your being.

Your body is very much like a recording machine, obediently receiving and faithfully indicating the thoughts that are persistently held in it. The body is made up of thoughts and is subject to those thoughts, continually feeding on and expressing the mental food you furnish it.

The nerves are the wires that transmit the mind's message to all parts of the body. Since all parts of the body contain brain cells, they carry out the words that have been spoken to them. Talking about nervousness and weakness will produce those corresponding conditions in the body. Talking about a weak stomach will make your stomach weak. Talking about a bad liver will fix that idea in your liver.

The usual conversations among people create ill health instead of good health, because of wrong words. Words of disease set in motion a disintegrating force that will eventually shatter the strongest organism, if they are not neutralized by constructive words. Destructive words cause endless ills in one's mind, body and relationships. People who continually talk about disease invariably experience it.

Continual criticism produces rheumatism. Critical, inharmonious words cause unnatural deposits in the blood, which settle in the joints. Unforgiveness is a prolific cause of ill health. It will harden arteries and the liver, and affect the eyesight.

When a word is spoken, a chemical change takes place in the body. Because of this, the body may be renewed, even transformed, through the spoken word!

Repetition of any word fixes it in mind and causes it to become a moving force in the body. Thus the power of repeating good, life-filled words for health and strength.

Affirmation is your "yes" power for healing. To "affirm" means to "make firm." Whatever words you constantly repeat, you are making firm in your mind and body. Emerson realized this when he wrote: "Every opinion reacts on him who utters it."

To affirm means to assert positively, even in the face of all contrary evidence, that a thing is so. Through affirmation you are not changing God, Who is immutable good. Through affirmation you change your thinking, so that you may accept that immutable good in whatever form you decree.

As you affirm words of life, health, strength, you are saying "yes" to good health, even in the face of illness. Your spoken words are then recorded in your body, and health begins to manifest. *The great healers of old found that the practice of deliberately speaking constructive words guided them most quickly into the secret of healing.*

AFFIRMATION HEALS TUBERCULOSIS

Myrtle Fillmore was a Kansas City wife, mother and former schoolteacher of the Methodist faith, who proved the healing power of affirmation in her own life. In 1886, Mrs. Fillmore learned that she had tuberculosis, which was considered an incurable disease. She was given six months to live.

One spring night, her husband took her to attend a metaphysical lecture. Having had a traditional religious backgound, the Fillmores knew nothing of the power of thought to heal, but were desperately willing to consider any constructive technique that might restore health.

At the lecture the speaker said, "You are a child of God, therefore you do not inherit sickness." This was an electrifying idea to Mrs. Fillmore, who had been led to believe that she had probably inherited tuberculosis, a further reason why nothing could be done for her.

She personally describes how she was healed through affirmation:

> I have made what seems to me a discovery. I was fearfully sick; I had all the ills of mind and body that I could bear. Medicine and doctors ceased to give me relief, and I was in despair when I found practical Christianity. I took it up and I was healed. I did most of the healing myself, because I wanted the understanding for future use. This is how I made what I call my discovery.
>
> I was thinking about life. Life is everywhere—in worm and in man. "Then why does not the life in the worm make a body like man's?" I asked. Then I thought, "The worm has not as much sense as a man." Ah! Intelligence, as well as life, is needed to make a body. Here is the key to my discovery. Life has to be guided by intelligence in making all forms. The same law works in my own body.
>
> Life is simply a form of energy, and has to be guided and directed in man's body by his intelligence. How do we communicate with intelligence? By thinking and talking, of course. Then it flashed upon me that I might talk to the life in every part of my body and have it do just what I wanted. I began to teach my body and got marvelous results.
>
> I told the life in my liver that it was not torpid or inert, but full of vigor and energy. I told the life in my stomach that it was not weak or inefficient, but energetic, strong, and intelligent. I told the life in my ab-

domen that it was no longer infested with ignorant thoughts of disease . . . but that it was all athrill with the sweet, pure, wholesome energy of God. I told my limbs that they were active and strong.

I went to all the life centers in my body and spoke words of Truth to them—words of strength and power. I asked their forgiveness for the foolish, ignorant course that I had pursued in the past, when I had condemned them and called them weak, inefficient, and diseased. I did not become discouraged at their being slow to wake up, but kept right on, both silently and aloud, declaring words of Truth, until the organs responded.[1]

Immediately her health improved. Within two years, Myrtle Fillmore was completely well again and lived another forty years. She became a noted spiritual healer and later co-founded Unity, which has become a far-flung healing movement.

She proved that affirmation is the working power of God; that affirmations are far stronger than the strongest visible thing in the world, when rightly used. She proved that by affirmative words, you claim and appropriate that which is yours by divine right; and that words charged with power and intelligence increase with use. Scientists have substantiated her ideas that the body, as well as the universe, is filled with intelligence.

Through taking a statement filled with good words and declaring it over and over, man gains conscious attention of the innate intelligence, already actively at work through the subconscious functions of the cells and organs of his body.

---

1. From the book *The Story of Unity*, by James Dillet Freeman, published by Unity Books, Unity Village, MO 64065.

As man continues to speak good words, that innate intelligence is accelerated in its power to respond with positive results. The body is the obedient servant of the mind and plastic to man's thoughts and words. The body feeds on and builds according to man's thoughts and words. When these words are uplifting, they are life-giving. Through deliberate affirmations of health, man can claim and appropriate the life and vitality that are his divine heritage.

THE AUTHOR'S HEALING EXPERIENCES WITH AFFIRMATIONS

I shall never forget how overjoyed I was to learn of the healing power of affimations. Ill health had plagued me since childhood and I had assumed it was one of those unpleasant experiences that I would have to tolerate for life. Through daily use of affirmations, my chronic bad health began to improve. Finally a very serious health problem disappeared, though my family doctor had insisted that only major surgery could help. Many years have passed since I began using affirmations. They have transformed my health and my life.

Not only can we use affirmations to heal ourselves but also to help others. Our affirmations go where we send them. If you call the name "John Brown," he will subconsciously hear you, even though he is miles away. If you tell him over and over exactly what you want him to know, he will subconsciously respond. If your words are constructive, describing his innate life, health, vitality, he will brighten up and recover. This simple method of affirmative prayer has long been known and practiced as "absent treatment."

Affirmative prayer is one of the most powerful forms of intercessory prayer for others. I first discovered this when my son was small and quite ill. Medication brought no relief. He had a high fever and was unable to retain nourishment. I became concerned when I realized that he was not improving but was steadily growing weaker.

Circumstances did not leave me free at that time to mention affirmative prayer as a means of healing to those about me. The suggestion would have been considered ridiculous. As I prayed for guidance, it came to me to leave my son in the care of others and to go apart and pray. It seemed a heartless thing to do, since he was most fretful and uncomfortable. But I knew that my human love was not enough to heal him.

I remained alone for a day, taking with me several books on healing, and the Bible, from which I read uplifting statements about healing, and from which I affirmed health-filled affirmations over and over. Toward mid-afternoon I had a feeling that the crisis had passed and that my son was going to be all right. From that point on, I simply gave thanks for his healing. That night when I walked into the house, he called out in a strong voice, "Mother!" His fever was gone and he had received nourishment for the first time in days.

Another early experience in the healing power of affirmation occurred when I was visiting an elderly lady, who was interested in spiritual healing. On one of my weekly visits I had a cold and a cough. She seemed somewhat disappointed that I was not manifesting the ideas of healing which I was trying to impart to her through my visits. The next week I hesitated to visit her because I had not demonstrated healing of that cold, which had now developed into an even deeper cough. Having had a busy, challenging week, some-how I had not taken the time to pray for my own healing.

However, as I thought about whether I should see her that week, I had a strong conviction that I should — cold or no cold. When I appeared, she was obviously disappointed to see that I still was suffering. Little was said about it, though, as we began discussing a book on healing.

Later, as was our practice, we began to pray aloud affirmatively. When we first began making affirma-tions, I could not breathe freely. The words came with great effort and discomfort, but the more affirmations we decreed, the easier I breathed. Finally I realized that I was breathing freely for the first time in days and that my throat was beginning to feel comfortable. As we continued our affirmative prayers, I felt a warm flow of life permeate my body. When this occurred, it was as though a heavy burden had passed away. And it had. I had been healed! Needless to say, this friend's witnessing my healing through affirmations did far more for her faith in its power than all our previous discussions.

AFFIRMATION HELPS "CHANGE OF LIFE"

A woman going through the "change of life" learned of the protective power of affirmation in the face of unsettling experiences. One night when she was in great pain and seemed unable to control the functions of her body, she affirmed over and over many times: "I GIVE THANKS THAT MY LIFE FORCES ARE NOW CON-SERVED AND CONTROLLED. I GIVE THANKS FOR THE OR-

DERLY ADJUSTMENT OF EVERY FUNCTION OF MY BODY. I AM STRENGTHENED, RENEWED, HEALED." Within a short time the pain was gone. Order was established and maintained in her body as the menopause experience was completed uneventfully.

A TOOTHACHE IS HEALED

A businessman was suffering from a toothache, which dental treatment had not alleviated. Pain-relieving drugs had only made him nauseous. One day, in much pain, he remained home from work and decided to try the healing power of affirmation, about which he had recently learned. Over and over he affirmed for the pain and swelling: "I AM THE RADIANT CHILD OF GOD. MY MIND, BODY, AND AFFAIRS NOW EXPRESS HIS RADIANT PERFECTION." He surely did not feel radiant as he began affirming these words, but gradually he began to feel better.

By mid-afternoon, the pain was entirely gone and the swelling was subsiding. That night he rested peacefully for the first time in several nights, and he returned to work refreshed the next day.

SMOKING HABIT IS CONQUERED

A couple who knew of the healing power of affirmations decided to use them for the husband's smoking habit, which was affecting his health. They decided it would be easier for his subconscious mind to accept the suggestion that he no longer cared to smoke, if that suggestion was given impersonally by someone other than himself.

Each night he would lie down and relax. Nearby, his wife would sit quietly and affirm for him: "YOU NO LONGER DESIRE TO SMOKE. YOU HAVE LOST ALL DESIRE FOR SMOKING. IT HAS NO APPEAL FOR YOU. THE SMOKING DESIRE HAS LEFT YOU. YOU CAN NO LONGER SMOKE. IT DOES NOT TASTE RIGHT AND HAS NO APPEAL TO YOU." After only a few days, his desire for cigarettes began to diminish. Within a few weeks, he had lost all interest in smoking.

An unexpected occurrence was this: As his wife affirmed these affirmations for her husband, they also worked for her! She found that she soon had no desire to smoke either.

SEA CAPTAIN HEALS HIMSELF OF ALCOHOLISM

The ancient Greeks believed that health was an entity that would come by being called. Some years ago, I met a man who proved this theory. Through affirmations, he healed himself of alcoholism when all human methods had failed.

This man was a sea captain who began to drink during many lonely hours spent at sea. Finally, he realized that he had become an alcoholic. Every time his ship docked, he would seek help for his problem. Though he sometimes found temporary relief, nothing he tried brought a permanent healing.

One day aboard ship, he found a publication that mentioned affirmative prayer as a scientific, practical, and easy way to contact God and His healing power. In desperation, this sea captain decided to try it.

This man told me that he made his mind start working for him instead of against him, by feeding it strong, affirmative statements that acknowledged the presence and power of God's goodness in the midst of his drinking problem. The first statement he began affirming over and over daily was: "ALCOHOLICS CAN BE HEALED!" The next statement he affirmed over and over was: "I AM BEING HEALED! YES, IT IS TRUE. RIGHT NOW, AT THIS VERY MOMENT. GOD IS HEALING ME OF THE DESIRE FOR STRONG DRINK." He carried these statements mentally with him for a number of days.

Later, he added the following to his repertory: "I REALIZE THAT I CAN BE HEALED BECAUSE WITH GOD ALL GOOD THINGS ARE POSSIBLE. I KNOW, TOO, THAT GOD WANTS ME TO BE HEALED BECAUSE I AM HIS CHILD AND HE LOVES ME. IN THE ASSURANCE THAT I AM BEING HEALED, I SURRENDER MY LIFE AND ITS PROBLEMS TO THE ALL-KNOWING MIND OF GOD. NOT ONLY AM I BEING HEALED OF THE DESIRE FOR STRONG DRINK, I AM BEING RELIEVED OF THE BURDENS OF ILL HEALTH, FINANCIAL DIFFICULTIES, FEAR, AND RESENTMENT. I AM BEING TRANSFORMED WITHIN AND WITHOUT! I AM HAPPY IN MY UNDERTAKING TO ATTAIN AND MAINTAIN SOBRIETY. I NOW LAUNCH FORTH INTO A NEW WORLD WITH COURAGE, CONFIDENCE AND FAITH."

In due time this man graduated from the idea that he could be healed, to the idea that he *was* healed: "I AM HEALED! YES, THANK GOD, IT IS TRUE! I AM NOW HEALED OF THE DESIRE FOR STRONG DRINK. I AM HAPPY AND THRILLED WITH THIS NEW WAY OF LIFE. MY JOY IS FULL. THE POWER OF GOD SUSTAINS AND PROTECTS ME AGAINST ALL MENTAL AND PHYSICAL TEMPTATION. MY

SOBRIETY NOW PAYS ME ENORMOUS DIVIDENDS IN HEALTH, WEALTH, AND HAPPINESS. GOOD RETURNS TO ME A THOUSANDFOLD."

In the last phase of his rehabilitation through affirmative prayer he declared: "THERE ARE NO OFF DAYS, NO DULL DAYS IN THIS NEW WAY OF THINKING AND LIVING. EVERY HOUR OF WHOLENESS IS ONE OF JOYOUS EXCITEMENT AND ADVENTURE. I RISE TO NEW HEIGHTS EVERY DAY. THIS I ACCEPT, THIS I BELIEVE. I THANK YOU, DEAR GOD, FOR THIS COMPLETE AND PERMANENT HEALING."

At the time I talked with this man he was well and happy and had been sober for a number of years. I continued to hear from him during his lifetime, and his healing was complete. He often helped others to use this same technique for healing.

HOW AFFIRMATIONS HAVE HEALED OTHERS

Healing through affirmative prayer is legend. In 1944 a young businessman lay in a coma in a New York hospital, given up to die. His wife sat by his bed, holding a card containing *The Prayer of Faith* (by H. M. Kohaus.[2] From that card she used the affirmation for her husband: "GOD IS YOUR HEALTH, YOU CAN'T BE SICK. GOD IS YOUR STRENGTH, UNFAILING QUICK!" Her husband recovered, later studied for the ministry, and now serves as a Unity minister.

I once had occasion to attend some of the mid-week healing services at a beautiful new church. This church was dedicated "to the healing ministry of Jesus

---

2. Printed by Unity School of Christianity, Unity Village, MO 64065.

Christ." Through his mid-week healing services, the minister has been a channel of healing to many.

A former businessman, this minister considered becoming a medical doctor and went so far as to take the pre-medical courses in college. The son of a chiropractor, he had always been interested in healing. After a thorough study of the Bible, he became interested in spiritual healing, and resolved to dedicate his life to it.

In his healing services, this minister constantly affirms to the congregation that God's will for them is healing. He gives a short sermon based upon some account of healing from the Bible. The congregation joins him in songs that affirm health. He prays affirmatively for them as a group. He then invites them to the altar to receive a special healing blessing. At the altar he practices the Biblical healing method of laying on of hands, praying for each one individually. His advice is: "Do not expect God to do it all. Pray to Him, then do something in faith."

The act of making the effort to get to the altar seems to be the "something in faith" that leads many to healing. One has only to talk to those who attend his services to find that his healing methods work.

I talked with a businessman whose healing was recorded in an unsolicited letter he had written this minister:

> For nine weeks I lay in the hospital gravely ill, having suffered many severe heart attacks. Through your frequent visits, you taught me to rely on God for my healing. When the finest doctors in the city told my family they had done all they could for me and that only a miracle beyond medicine could save my life, you appeared at a very critical moment when I was having a severe heart attack, barely able to breathe.

You laid your hands on me and prayed affirmatively that I would be healed. As you did so, I felt as if a hot poker was moving up through my left arm and across my chest. Thereafter, I was able to breathe deeply and easily, as the pain began leaving me. Just three days later I was released from the hospital!

It is not possible for me to put into words the change which that healing has made in my thinking and in my entire way of life. Not only have I been blessed but other members of my family have been healed of various illnesses, since that time, through your help. It is my sincere wish that many more will be helped, as much as my family and I have been, through coming to know and use the power of affirmative prayer.

A lady lay in her hospital bed, suffering from cancer of the liver. She was not expected to live through the night. As she was going in and out of consciousness, she could dimly see a clerical collar and knew this same minister was there praying for her. As he prayed affirmatively, decreeing God's will was health and wholeness for her, she relaxed into a deep, peaceful sleep. The next day, when this minister returned, he found her sitting in the lounge, relaxed and happy. A healing had taken place.

The church organist had suffered from a tumor on one finger, the size of a marble. Over a matter of months, it continued to grow. After one night's healing services in which she had joined in affirmative prayer for healing, she prayed, "God, show me what to do to get a healing." The next day, as she was walking from one room to another, she felt severe pain go from the fingertips through the shoulder. The tumor had disappeared.

A housewife attended services at this minister's church one night, after having hurt her hand. She merely said to him, "I caught my hand in the car door today." Then extending her hand toward him she said, "Heal it." Taking her hand, he affirmed, "It is healed." According to a letter she later wrote him, it was. No discolored nails, no signs of a bruise, no discomfort remained in any way. She reported: "It was an instantaneous healing."

AN ANCIENT TEACHING FOR MODERN USE

That your words have unlimited power has been a Truth known since ancient times. Primitive man used affirmations through incantation. When there was a healing need, the priest-medicine man was called to speak words of healing.

The Babylonians taught that a word is either a command or a promise which is bound to come true. That the word is all powerful is a prevalent teaching in the ancient Hindu Scriptures. The Greeks have taught down through the centuries that the word is substance itself, containing a cosmic power with which you can do anything—build up or tear down.

The Oriental races have long taught that through the dynamics of sound, every word spoken has tremendous power; and that by certain arrangements of words—such as in healing affirmations—a tremendous vibratory force can be set up in the invisible which profoundly affects physical substance.

The Egyptian priests of old, by means of affirmative chants, set up strong vibratory forces which dissolved congestions in the body, and which even assisted Nature in reconstructing broken bones or depleted

organs. The priests knew that by their persistent healing chants, they greatly stimulated centers of consciousness which are located in the body, thus deliberately causing healing to occur. *They constantly
proved that mind power in the body is aroused and
called into healing action through affirmation.*

The ancient Egyptian scriptures, whose creation
story is similar to our Genesis version, emphasized the
power of the word. Their scriptures state the world was
made when their gods "spoke it into existence." They
believed that whatever "flows from your mouth happens" and "that which you speak comes into being."

Our own Genesis creation story emphasizes this:
"God said, 'Let there be . . . and there was.'" (Genesis
1) Our Holy Bible points out repeatedly that man's
word contains great power. The Psalmist said, "He
sent his word and healed them." (Psalms 107:20)
The prophet, Joel, advised: "Let the weak say, 'I am
strong.'" (Joel 3:10)

Solomon often talked about the power of words to
kill or cure: "Death and life are in the power of the
tongue." (Proverbs 18:21) "He that guardeth his
mouth keepeth his life." (Proverbs 13:3) "Pleasant
words are as a honeycomb, sweet to the soul and
health to the bones." (Proverbs 16:24) "The tongue of
the wise is health." (Proverbs 12:18)

Jesus did all things by his word: Healed the sick,
raised the dead, stilled the storm, fed the multitude.
What he did, he claimed that we might do. The cen-
turion recognized the healing power of words when he
asked of Jesus: "Speak the word only, and my servant
shall be healed." (Matthew 8:8) Jesus' spoken words
that healed the servant were: "'As thou hast believed,
so be it done unto thee.' And the servant was healed in
that hour." (Matthew 8:13)

HEALING THROUGH WRITTEN WORDS

The ancient Chinese believed words were so power-ful that no piece of paper containing written words should ever be destroyed, even when it was no longer of value.

If at times you do not have the privacy needed for speaking forth your affirmations, then write them down on paper. There is something about the written word that reaches past one's fears and anxieties and makes an indelible impression for good upon the mind, leading to happy results. Write down what you would like your body to do and be. Read over your healing words at intervals. When possible, read them aloud. Many a case of sickness would be healed if more people would write out their healing ideas and pri-vately read them over and over. Through written af-firmations, you can quietly accomplish much.

A FORMULA FOR HEALTH

In India, it is both legend and tradition that the sung or spoken word has more power and influence than anything else in existence.

Some modern metaphysicians would agree, as they claim that the spoken or sung word is 80 percent more powerful than the silent word.

A Protestant minister, who was known as "the poor man's psychiatrist" in his city, because of his tremen-dous success in pastoral counseling, once told me that for many years he studied and experimented with every healing technique advocated by modern psychology. After testing every method including "deep analysis," which is used by psychoanalysts, this popular minister discovered that the simple technique of affirmative prayer was far more effective and quicker in healing those who came to him with their problems. His discovery of the healing power of affirmation made it possible for him to see countless more people, and to introduce them to affirmations, so that they could immediately begin to help themselves. His phenomenal success provided a great tribute to the healing power of the spoken word.

A simple formula for invoking healing through affirmation is this:

Take a statement that expresses life, health, wholeness, and declare it over and over. This statement can be a Bible promise or some other healing affirmation that appeals to you. It does not matter that at first you do not believe the statement, or do not see how it can come true. If you will persistently affirm it anyway, even though it seems hard to mentally accept, you will find that your affirmations have power. Daily affirm and yet affirm once more. Your persistent affirmations will uplift your conscious thinking, which in turn, will change your subconscious feeling nature. Since the subconscious controls the body as it changes, so changes the body.

As you study the next several chapters describing various types of affirmations that are especially powerful for healing, you will doubtless find the type that is just right for you. Meanwhile, you can begin invoking the "yes" law of healing by affirming: "LET THERE BE HEALTH IN MY MIND AND BODY, AND WHOLENESS THROUGHOUT MY LIFE NOW."

THE HEALING LAW
OF PRAISE

— Chapter 6 —

The expression of praise as thanksgiving, gratitude and joy is among the most powerful forms of affirmation.

If you wait to be healed before you express thanksgiving, you may wait indefinitely! *One of the greatest secrets of healing is to praise and give thanks for it, right in the face of illness, before there is anything to give thanks for!*

The reason praise is so powerful for healing is this: What you praise you increase. Praise liberates and releases the life force that is pent up in the atoms of your body.

Words that express gratitude, praise and thanksgiving release certain potent energies of mind and body that are not otherwise tapped. Praise also liberates the

97

finer essences of the soul that are necessary for a complete healing. Through praise and thanksgiving, you activate the dynamic powers of the subconscious and superconscious phases of your being, which act speedily for your improved health.

You can praise yourself from weakness to strength, from ignorance to intelligence, from poverty to affluence, from sickness to health.

I first became aware of the almost unbelievable power of praise through reading a testimonial written by a housewife:

> Surely no one knows better than I the potency of praise. Before I came to this understanding I was a chronic grumbler and the whole atmosphere about me was steeped with fault-finding and complaining. Praise eliminated pain from my body and trouble from my mind. Since I have adopted the praise method, there has also been a great change in all my household, especially in my domestic help and in the children.

HOW PRAISE HEALS

It is possible for persistent praise to make a complete change in one's health and appearance.

One cannot fail to experience improved health, if his thoughts and words are filled with praise, never yielding to condemnation. Pliny, the Roman statesman, wrote that some people carry health in their presence as a result of praise-filled words. For centuries mankind has been urged by both Hebrew and Hindu philosophers to invoke the potent power of praise. You open the way for great demonstrations through praise and thanksgiving.

A frustrated woman had become a mental and physical wreck through dwelling upon her problems. As she continually talked about her aches and pains, they multiplied. She had proved that what you give your attention to increases.

The despair of all the doctors who had tried to help her, she finally sought spiritual healing. While listening to this woman's long list of woes, the spiritual counselor decided that along with everything else this lady claimed was wrong with her, she had one disease she had overlooked: She was also a hypochondriac.

Finally the counselor interrupted her: "Now that you have told me all that is wrong with you, tell me something that is right with you."

Almost in anger the sick woman declared there was nothing right in her health. The counselor persisted: "There must be. You are able to walk, talk, see, hear, taste, smell. You are not bedridden or helpless. You are enjoying some degree of health, or you would not be here."

Reluctantly the woman agreed that there *was* one thing that was right in her health: Her little finger was perfect!

The counselor told this whining woman to go home and for three days to concentrate on the perfection in that little finger; to praise its health, to thank God for its life and wholeness; and to refuse to speak of her ills.

Three days later the woman returned. This time she reluctantly agreed that her health was improving. Not only was there nothing wrong with her little finger, but now her whole right hand was well! Again she was sent home to praise the increased health found there.

As the counselor kept working with her, the woman finally agreed that she was completely healed.

When you are tempted to recite your ills, remember this lady. Find something that you can praise. Be thankful for it and your health will improve. You might begin by affirming: "I PRAISE WHAT STRENGTH I HAVE; I GIVE THANKS FOR WHAT HEALTH I HAVE; I GLORY IN WHAT LIFE I HAVE; AND GOD NOW GIVES THE IN-CREASE!"

The late Dr. Ernest Holmes of Los Angeles, founder of the Religious Science movement,[1] whose philosophy has healed countless people, once related an experience in the healing power of praise. He met a healthy, vital woman of sixty, who told him that only a year before, at the age of fifty-nine, she had been a hopeless cripple, suffering from painful arthritis.

When Dr. Holmes asked her healing secret, she replied: "I made up my mind that there is an intelligent principle everywhere in the universe. It flows through me and I can talk to it. I began to praise it and to tell each joint in my body what I wanted it to do, and how wonderful I thought it was." Within a year she had been completely healed.

The noted Japanese metaphysician, Dr. Masaharu Taniguchi, has been especially successful in the healing of cancer. In his book, *You Can Heal Yourself*,[2] he gives his secret: "These ideas of 'Forgive me,' and 'Thank you' cure all diseases." He explains that thanksgiving neutralizes stress and leads to the cure of disease.

---

1. Worldwide headquarters for the Religious Science movement is located at 3251 West 6th Street, Los Angeles, CA 90075.

2. Published by Seicho-no-Ie Foundation, Divine Publication Dept., Akasaka Hinoki-Cho, Minato-ku, Tokyo, Japan.

People of the Orient have long known of the healing power of praise and thanksgiving. Many years ago, a young Japanese developed tuberculosis, which was considered as dreaded a disease as cancer has been in recent times.

As he learned the healing power of praise, he realized that his previous fault-finding, critical, complaining words had doubtlessly helped bring on his condition. Though it was hard not to continue complaining, he deliberately made himself do just the opposite and began to praise everything and everybody.

At first, the tuberculosis seemed to grow worse. (See chapter 12 on chemicalization). He paid no attention, as he kept on praising everything and everybody. One night when he felt as though he was breathing his last breath, he persisted in praising his body with perfect health.

Suddenly his breath grew deep and electrifying, after which he was able to straighten up and breathe easily. It had been an *instant healing*. The news quickly spread and as he invoked the power of praise for others, he became a spiritual healer.

THE HEALING POWER
OF SINGING AND LAUGHTER

Praise and thanksgiving open the way to restored health when nothing else will. In fact, many have proved that you do not need one thing more than you already have to experience a healing, if you know the law of praise and thanksgiving.

A middle-aged woman broke her wrist in such a way that it was necessary to insert a metal plate to aid in its healing. As her physician placed her wrist in a cast, he informed her that when it had healed, it would remain stiff; that she would not be able to move it, and that she should "reconcile" herself to this condition for life.

Instead of accepting that diagnosis, this lady wrote a little song of thanks which she sang daily: "Thank you, God, for my perfect arm, thank you, God. Thank you, God, for your perfect healing, thank you, God. Thank you, God, for the pain, thank you, God. Thank you, God, for perfection. This is my refrain, thank you, God."

When the cast was removed twelve weeks later, she immediately moved her wrist, with no pain or ill effects. Her doctor exclaimed that it was not "medically possible," but she did so anyway. That was in 1946. When this lady was well past middle age, she still moved her wrist easily with no discomfort.

In her book, *What Are You?*, Imelda Shanklin relates the story of a young man who ran from a burning house, his clothes in flames. As he ran, he tore the blazing garments from him. After staggering into a hospital, he was given the best attention, but the physicians said he could not recover from the burns that had seared more than one half of his body.

In bed, bandaged and suffering, the young man began to sing. The attendants said that he was rallying before transition. He sang on. Then they said that the singing was an expression of delirium caused by suffering. He continued to sing. It was then said that his singing was an effect of medicines administered. Still the young man sang, as he recovered. Later, his explanation for his healing was: "When I ran from the house with my clothes in flames, I determined to live.

I knew that if I could keep my thoughts on life, and could keep singing, I would recover."[3]

Charles Fillmore has explained in his book, *Jesus Christ Heals*:

> All healing systems recognize joy as a beneficent factor in the restoration of health to the sick. An old country doctor used to tell how he healed a woman of a large cyst by telling her a funny story, at which she laughed so heartily that the fluid broke loose and passed away. The mind puts kinks in the nerves in ways beyond description. A thought of fear will stop the even flow of life in some nerve center deep down in the body, forming a nucleus where other fears may accumulate and finally congest the blood concerned in some important function. The impact of energy of some kind is necessary to break the dam.
>
> There are various methods of erasing fear from the mind and preventing its congestions in the body. One of the most direct and effective shatterers of fear is laughter. Laugh away your fears. See how ridiculous they are when traced to their source.
>
> That there is an intimate relation between happiness and health goes without question. Singing promotes health because it increases the circulation, and good circulation is a sign and promoter of health. If the bloodstream were never congested and all the nerves and pores were open, free and swiftly carrying forward their appointed work, there would never be an abnormal or false growth in the body. It follows logically, then, that we should cultivate those mind activities which naturally stimulate the currents of life in our body. One of these, and a very important one, is joy.[4]

3. Published by Unity School of Christianity, Unity Village, MO 64065.

4. Published by Unity Books, Unity Village, MO 64065.

A lady who was prone to fits of depression, conquered them by forcing herself to sing bright, joyous songs and to play lively little tunes on the piano.

Another woman had experienced great sorrow in her life and had fallen victim to despondency and insomnia. Finally her physician informed her she would have to overcome her despondency which was affecting her health. He advised that the way to conquer it was to laugh at least three times a day, whether she felt like it or not.

Though it seemed ridiculous advice, she retired to her room three times daily for the sole purpose of laughing and making merry. Soon she was in excellent health again, and her previously sorrowful life took on happy new experiences.

A businessman wanted to stop smoking, because it was affecting his throat. He had tried everything. Finally a friend suggested he go to the piano each day, play and sing over and over some happy, affirmative song. This he did and the desire to smoke vanished. In the singing process, he also regained the fine trained voice he had once used for professional entertaining. Healing through song is a powerful form of affirmation, since the healing vibration is intensified as much as 80 percent.

MAKE FUN YOUR MEDICINE

If people only knew the healing power of laughter and joy, many of our fine doctors would be out of business. Joy is one of nature's greatest medicines. Joy is always healthful. *A pleasant state of mind tends to bring abnormal conditions back to normal.* People who keep themselves in physical and mental harmony through laughter, pleasantness, and joy usually live longer and are healthier than those who take themselves or events too seriously. *Many diseases come from the lack of expressing joy.*

When you feel you cannot go on, make it a point to practice smiling. Smile at the pictures on the wall. Smile at the furniture. Smile until the tension has left your body, and you feel relaxed again.

A physician once stated that fun is a food that is necessary to your health as bread and water. *A complete revolution takes place in your physical and mental being when you've laughed and had some fun.* Too many people grow stale mentally, emotionally, and physically because they have forgotten the importance of laughing and being pleasant.

GRATITUDE HEALS RESENTMENT

Many physical ills and certainly most mental ills are due, consciously or unconsciously, to feelings of resentment. *You cannot be grateful and resentful at the same time.* When you feel a surge of resentment because of some slight, hurt, or disappointment, deliberately change the direction of your feelings by thinking of something for which you are grateful. As you do, you will find that you can be grateful for the experience that previously made you resentful, since that resentment finally caused you to cultivate the praiseful, thankful, grateful state of mind.

Make a practice of praising your problems, troubles and difficult experiences. Any experience that leads you to a deeper degree of good should be praised.

Every sorrow, disappointment and hard experience is trying to lead you to greater understanding, which, in turn, leads to a better way of life. *Therefore, your hard experiences should be praised.* They are a blessing in disguise. According to a fifteenth-century mystic, there is a radiance, a glory, shining forth in our dark experiences, could we but see it.

One housewife's formula for meeting dark experiences is this: "I have learned that I can always resort to the act of thanksgiving with good results. No matter what the situation, the words 'Thank you, God' open the way for better living. Health, prosperity, and peace come when one begins thanking God in the face of dark experiences."

PRAISE BRINGS VICTORY

The Hebrews were shown, during their wilderness wanderings, that their suffering and afflictions came, not because God had willed it, but because they had been disobedient to the law of praise: "All these curses shall come upon thee, and shall pursue thee, and overtake thee. . . . Because thou servedst not Jehovah thy God with joyfulness, and with gladness of heart, by reason of the abundance of all things." (Deuteronomy 28:15,47)

That the Hebrews heeded this advice and turned to the law of praise is evidenced in their later victories. From the time of Joshua on, the Old Testament is filled with illustrations in which the Hebrews went forth in small numbers to meet a mighty enemy in battle and were victorious.[5] When meeting the enemy host of Moabites and Ammonites, Jehoshaphat appointed singers to go before his soldiers chanting songs of praise and thanksgiving. They were the winners. (II Chronicles 20:20–28) "Praise ye Jehovah," was the constant refrain of the Psalmist, who, at one point, vowed: "Seven times a day do I praise thee." (Psalms 119:164)

The ancients believed that one person singing and speaking words of praise had more power than ten people who were not. The Hebrews proved it. Praise was their favorite method of prayer. In the Old Testament, prayer in the form of "bowing down" appears only three times; prayer as a "petition", "entreaty", or as an "asking" appears only five times; prayer as "meditation" is used only twice. But the other word, translated seventy-six times as prayer is to "sing and dance in praise of the Lord for the things He is giving you." To the Hebrews, prayer was an attitude of song, dance, and praise!

THE ACTIVATING POWER OF PRAISE

A discouraged woman once saw a little placard that read, "Praise the Lord anyhow." She began to use those words as a daily affirmation. Later she said, "When I remember to practice the law of praise, unpleasantness magically disappears. If I have difficulty getting to sleep at night, I speak words of praise, and the next thing I know, it is morning and I have rested

5. See the author's books, *The Millionaire Moses,* and *The Millionaire Joshua.*

well. If I have pain and can remember to praise the
Lord anyhow, it is startling how quickly I feel better.
What happens to the pain? How should I know? I have
been too busy speaking words of praise to know when it
left."

*Praise and thanksgiving activate life in the cells of
the body, releasing increased amounts of energy and
restoring wholeness.*

A secretary had suffered constant pain from a
chronic health problem for twenty years, after having
sought many types of help, to no avail. Late one afternoon, she was walking slowly across a long bridge that
gave her a beautiful view of the sunset. As she silently
marveled at that glorious view, a sense of exhilaration
came over her, and suddenly, the torturous pain of
twenty years was gone. It was a complete healing.

There is always something you can praise. As you
do, your own good multiplies.

Perhaps you've heard the story of the little boy who
believed in the restoring power of praise. He arrived
home one day from school leading a stray dog, which
he proudly showed off to his mother. But she was un-
impressed, as she said, "Where did you find that awful-
looking old mutt?"

"He's not awful looking. He's a wonderful dog," her
son replied.

"That mangy, flea-bitten hound? Why son, he can't
even stand up."

"Yes, but Mother, look how nicely he can wag his
tail."

A mother had an only son who had begun to drink
heavily. For months she prayed, "Oh God, save my boy
from destruction, sin and death." But nothing happened. Finally this mother stopped beseeching God to

save her son and she said to herself, "I will give thanks instead."

She did not say one word to her son in rebuke, nor did she tell him she was praying for him. Still he drank; still she continued giving thanks for his healing. After a few weeks of no apparent change, one night her son came home and said, "Mother, I am tired of living this kind of life. I am going to stop being a drunkard and start being a man." And he did.

Jesus used this healing technique for raising Lazarus from the dead. His first act was one of thanksgiving: "Father, I thank thee that thou hast heard me. And I knew that thou hearest me always." (John 11:41,42)

PRAISE HEALS THE SICK POCKETBOOK

A sick pocketbook also responds to the healing law of praise and thanksgiving.

People sometimes neglect to give thanks and feel grateful for so long that things get very bad for them. We have all had hardships because we neglected "the attitude of gratitude." *If you are having financial problems, it is probably because you have been ungrateful and cynical. There is nothing that will empty your pocketbook and bank account more quickly than the cynical, ungrateful state of mind.* There is an old proverb: "The ungrateful never escape."

If you have certain challenges in your life which you have been unable to escape, check your attitudes to see if you have not become ungrateful. So long as you remain cynical, you will never escape those challenges. They will only multiply. Conversely, when you cast off bitterness and resentment through invoking the almighty power of praise, your bounty will increase.

A businesswoman recently proved this. She had had extra expenses, the payment of which was due, plus the payment of current bills. There was not nearly enough money to go around.

She had affirmed and affirmed that there would be adequate supply, but nothing happened. Then she realized she had gotten cynical, criticizing her bills, and condemning her inability to pay them. She had also criticized the unexpected experiences that had brought on the additional expense. Furthermore, she had even condemned her usual channels of supply, saying they were insufficient. After those strong words, her supply had literally "dried up," and prosperity had avoided her on every hand.

Now realizing her error, she went into a room alone, and began privately to speak words of praise. Taking in her hands the bills that were due, she affirmed: "I PRAISE YOU AS THE PERFECT CREATION OF DIVINE BOUNTY NOW." Hanging in the closet were clothes not yet paid for. Placing her hands on them she said: "I PRAISE YOU AS THE PERFECT CREATION OF DIVINE BOUNTY NOW." The light and water bills were due. She went to a table lamp, turned on the light, and placing her hand on the warm bulb, affirmed: "I PRAISE YOU AS THE PERFECT CREATION OF DIVINE BOUNTY NOW." Next, she turned on the water faucet, and letting the water pour over her hand, made the same affirmation.

She then went to the refrigerator, which was almost empty, opened it and used the same affirmation. Placing her hands on the empty pantry shelves, she did the same thing. Since the rent was due, she also placed her hands on the walls of her home and again made the affirmation. Taking her wallet and checkbook in her hands, she affirmed divine bounty for them, too.

For at least an hour she spoke forth this affirmation of praise for every phase of her financial world. An elated feeling of excitement and expectancy of good came over her.

Within another hour, the telephone rang. It was a long-distance caller offering her special work which she was to do immediately. This work would not interfere with her usual work and because of the necessity for its immediate accomplishment, it would pay her the equivalent of a month's pay on her usual job! With this sudden doubled income, she was able to meet her financial obligations. *With praise and thanksgiving, every obstacle can be overcome.* She proved it.

CRITICISM IS PRAISE OF THE NEGATIVE

You have no idea how much suffering and disease is caused in the life of a person who dwells on the wrong-doings of himself or others. I once met a man who had experienced two marvelous spiritual healings. One had occurred around 1930 at a time when this man was in the hospital, desperately ill with cancer. A spiritual healer came to the hospital, placed the Holy Bible on this man's body, and prayed for him. The cancer disappeared and he resumed a normal life.

Thirty years later, when he was again very ill — this time from painful, "incurable" arthritis — with great effort he managed to get to a healing service being conducted by a noted spiritual healer. As the healer asked those in the audience seeking health to rise, this crippled man struggled to do so. After painfully getting on his feet, he followed the healer's advice and prayed for a man standing nearby, who also sought healing.

After this two-hour healing service was over, this businessman realized that the pain in his aching joints was subsiding. He had been scheduled to leave town to get special medical treatment for arthritis. But the next morning he felt so much better, he remained at home. A few days later, he realized that the pain he had endured for many years was completely gone.

I witnessed this man's healing at this special service. The next week, as he informed me of his healing, he gave me the mental clue to why he had suffered so much over the years, in spite of an earlier healing. He criticized everything and everybody, even after this second marvelous healing. He was still busily fretting over what he considered the wrong-doings of others.

Recognition is a form of praise. Description is a form of praise. To describe and dwell upon what you do not like, magnifies its importance, and gives it negative power, which reacts upon you. Because of his critical attitudes, I wonder if this man maintained his second spiritual healing any better than he had maintained his first.

PERMANENT HEALING MAY BE SLOWER

Spiritual healers are sometimes criticized because those receiving their help do not maintain their healings. This is not the healer's fault. To receive a healing is one thing. To maintain it is quite another. Much

depends upon the mental attitude of the one being
healed.

Because mental attitudes are so important to
permanent health, often a healing that takes longer to
attain is more desirable. Through persistent prayer
and spiritual study, the disease-filled attitudes of hate,
fear, condemnation, guilt, forgiveness, and ingrati-
tude are gradually cleansed from mind and body.
Only as they are, is permanent healing possible.

A lady was once healed through spiritual study and
prayer. But she became proud and boastful of her
healing, and the old condition reappeared. When it
returned, she tried using prayers of denial and affirmation, to no avail. She read spiritual books and pub-
lications in an effort to find the answer, but still the
pain persisted.

One day as she was holding to healing affirmations,
the pain took an even firmer grip. Suddenly, in the
midst of this intense pain, the thought came to her
that *this pain was good*. Without the pain, she would
never have come into a deeper spiritual understanding. With this realization, a feeling of deep gratitude
and thanksgiving surged through her. In her ecstasy,
she forgot the pain. A little later she realized it was
gone. Thanksgiving had healed her.

As you pursue mental and spiritual methods of healing, if your healing takes longer than you anticipated,
then let it! A deeper healing may be taking place than
you had expected, which will be more permanent
and enduring than an instant healing might have
been. Thus in the face of apparent slowness in healing,
you can be thankful that a more thorough healing may
be occurring. Your thankfulness will help accelerate
that healing, and it will also help you to maintain it!

Never underestimate the power of praise. It is not only the master key to life, but one of the best antidotes for the world's ills. Begin to be quietly thankful, grateful, praiseful from the time you open your eyes in the morning until you close them at night. This practice will not only heal a sick body, but also a sick mind, sick relationships, and a sick pocketbook.

THE HEALING LAW
OF LOVE

— Chapter 7 —

Early in my ministry, I discovered that one type of affirmation often brought physical and emotional healings, when none other did. That type expressed divine love.

Disease often results from a violation of the law of love. Thoughts of hate generate a deadly poison in the body, which, if not neutralized, can even produce death. Love cleanses the mind and body of these hates that accumulate in the form of resentment, criticism, sorrow, remorse, guilt, fear, anger, jealousy. Affirmations of love change these killing thoughts into life thoughts. Affirmations of love bring peace to the mind and body.

Love has been described as the "physician of the universe," because it has the power to heal all ills, when invoked silently or by spoken affirmation.

115

Love is all-powerful because thoughts of love harmonize the mind. Love is also an awakener. Dwelling upon the phrase "divine love" awakens a positive current in the body, which will break up opposing thoughts of hate, rendering them and their destruction in the body, null and void. Love takes away all thoughts of destruction, as it levels all things into one harmonious whole. By a persistent cultivation of love, man can change his belief and rebuild his body cell by cell.

Emmet Fox has described the healing power of love in his book, *Power Through Constructive Thinking*:

> There is no difficulty that enough love will not conquer. There is no disease that enough love will not heal. . . . It makes no difference how deeply seated may be the trouble. It makes no difference how hopeless may be the outlook. . . . A sufficient realization of love will dissolve it all.[1]

Dr. Fox explains that unless you build up within yourself a love consciousness, all your other activities will be more or less futile; whereas when you develop a love consciousness toward all, everything else will follow.[2]

Dr. Fox states that many people have found very remarkable things happening in their lives after only a few days' special work done on love. All sorts of personal difficulties simply vanished away. As the months passed, their faces sometimes altered in a remarkable

1. Published by Harper & Bros., New York, N.Y., 1940.
2. Concerning how to develop a love consciousness, see the chapters on love in the author's books, *The Dynamic Laws of Prosperity, The Healing Secrets of the Ages, Open Your Mind to Prosperity* and *The Prospering Power of Love*.

way, since the body is usually the first thing to respond to freedom from fear and resentment. "People have told me that they have felt twenty years roll off their shoulders, after treating themselves a few days along these lines," he writes. And he concludes that to practice effectively the yoga of love is the quickest way to demonstrate over all your difficulties, as well as to help mankind universally demonstrate over its many troubles.

LOVE HEALS PAINFUL BURSITIS

Early in my ministry, I discovered the truth of Dr. Fox's words. Affirmations expressing divine love *are* among the most powerful type of prayers for healing.

A businesswoman had bursitis of the shoulder. She had been under medical care for several weeks, taking drugs and other treatments in an effort to relieve the pain. When the drugs wore off, the pain consistently returned. Finally her doctor told her there was nothing that could be done medically to cure bursitis and that she would have to endure the pain, hoping it would gradually subside.

One Sunday morning, after the church service, this lady asked my ministerial assistant and me to pray for her healing. In the church prayer room, the three of us gathered. My assistant and I verbally decreed for this woman: "DIVINE LOVE IS DOING ITS PERFECT WORK IN YOU AND THROUGH YOU NOW. YOU REST AND RELAX IN THE LOVE OF GOD, AND YOU ARE HEALED." For some time we made these affirmations and then silently meditated upon the healing power of divine love. At the conclusion of our prayer time, this lady went home with the instructions to take a nap. (This she had been unable to do for several weeks, because of the pain.) After resting, she was to telephone the results. Upon arriving home, she felt relaxed and drowsy. In spite of the pain, she was able to sleep, and when she awakened, the pain was gone. It did not return.

LOVE IS A MIND POWER

We often think of love as an emotion. We often think of love as a spiritual quality. It is both, but love is also a mind power native to man, existent in every one of us.

Certain words used persistently release this mind power to mold and transform conditions in the mind, body and affairs of man. The words "divine love" dissolve hate, resistance, opposition, obstinacy, anger, and other mental and physical frictions that cause pain and disease.

Words make cells and these cells adjust to each other through associated ideas. When the words "divine love" enter into man's thought processes, every cell responds with poise and balance. As it does, peace and harmony appear. Pain and disease fade away. By persistently dwelling upon the thought of "divine love," man unifies himself with the healing power of love within him, and it then pours forth through his body in healing streams. Through the thought of "divine love" man can free himself from all types of limitations.

LOVE HEALS HIGH FEVER AND
HEART CONDITION

Another experience witnessed early in my ministry convinced me of love's healing power:

I was called to the hospital to pray with a business-man who had a high fever, which his physicians had been unable to break up. Strong drugs would bring his fever down, but when the drug wore off, the fever returned. His condition seemed especially serious, because over a period of years he had suffered a chronic heart condition and had taken special drugs to arrest it. Any undue strain on his heart might bring dire results.

For some time this man had had marital difficulties, having gotten involved with "another woman." Instead of keeping quiet about their difficulties, his wife had talked loud and long to almost anyone who would listen. Her criticism had only exaggerated their problems. A complete gap had developed between them, followed by ill health, mounting financial problems, and unruly behavior in their insecure children. It seemed a deplorable situation.

As I stood by this man's hospital bed and affirmed for him: "GOD LOVES YOU, GOD IS GUIDING YOU, GOD IS SHOWING YOU THE WAY. YOU ARE BELOVED BY GOD AND MAN," tears came to his eyes and a sense of peace enveloped him.

Upon returning to my church study a few minutes later, a strange thing happened: As I sat down and relaxed, suddenly a feeling of intense heat passed through my body, followed by a burst of tears. The thought came, "This is an experience in vicarious healing. That man's high fever is passing through my body. I have just felt his own pent up anxieties as they have been released. He is being healed!"

The next morning his wife telephoned to confirm my belief. After our prayer the night before, all fever had left him. Within a few days he was released from the hospital, though he had spent several anxious weeks there. He began taking smaller and smaller doses of drugs. Later he threw away the medicines he had felt dependent upon for years. He remained a healthy, active man and lived a normal life span.

The original "heart trouble" connected with his marriage also cleared up, as his wife got quiet about their difficulties and began daily affirming for her husband and their marriage: "GOD LOVES YOU (US), GOD IS GUIDING YOU (US), GOD IS SHOWING YOU (US) THE WAY."

Thoughts of criticism and condemnation cause all kinds of illness. When you speak words of love, you clear up the negative emotion that caused the illness. Love is the greatest worker and will accomplish more for your happiness than all other mind powers combined. If you want a servant that will work for you night and day, cultivate divine love.

HOW TO TURN LOVE ON

Love is the key to healing. Many doctors now agree that the majority of man's ills come from congestion, and from poisons stirred up by negative emotions. Love relaxes and harmonizes man's emotions. Love attunes the individual to the healing power within himself.

Love is a faculty native to man, existent in every soul, which may be used to bring about harmony and unity among those who have been disunited through misunderstanding, contention, or selfishness. The ordinary man is not aware that he possesses this mighty power, which will turn away every shaft of hate that is aimed at him, and which will neutralize its destructive effect upon his body.

Some years ago, scientific studies on love at Harvard University, headed by Dr. Pitirim A. Sorokin, revealed that human beings have always placed love high on the list of things to be desired in life. But we have tended to look on love as something we could personally do little about. Love either happened to us or it didn't.

Now, thanks to that Harvard study, we are finding out otherwise. Love, like other good things, can be deliberately produced by human beings. There is no reason why we cannot learn to "generate" love as we do other natural forces.

The Harvard scientists discovered that you can actually bombard people, situations and conditions with love, thereby producing miraculous changes. They predicted that "turning love on" might soon become a universal prescription for healing the world's ills.

There is nothing new about these ideas on the power of love, though we delight in hearing them expressed by our eminent scientists. It was the Master Psychologist of the ages who informed the lawyer that love was the greatest of all the commandments. (Matthew 22: 35-40) One of the world's most profound intellectuals and builders of early Christianity, the Apostle Paul, also ascribed all power to love. (I Corinthians 13)

You can begin immediately "turning love on" in your life, thereby using it as a prescription for healing your ills. Make it a practice to meditate daily on the thought: "DIVINE LOVE, MANIFEST THYSELF IN ME." There should be periods of mental concentration on the love center in the cardiac plexus, near the heart. Think about love with the attention drawn within the breast, and a quickening will follow. All the ideas that go to make up love will be set in motion.

LOVE HEALS ARTHRITIS

Divine love has a balm for every ill. Violation of the law of love causes a short circuit in your health.

Resentment, hatred, envy, selfishness, and other negative emotions are responsible for most of man's diseases. Just as these strongly negative emotions affect the chemistry of the body, causing disease, so thoughts of love affect the chemistry of the body, producing restoration.

An elderly woman had been troubled for several years with arthritis. She could not use her fingers or hands. Most of the time the pain was unbearable, and her fists were doubled up. Trying to sleep was a nightmare. She sought out several doctors and applied their remedies, which helped some, but the pain always returned.

One day the Biblical promise, "Love never faileth," (I Corinthians 13:8) welled up in her thinking. She couldn't get that promise out of her mind. Then she read these words from a *Daily Word*:[3] "MY HEART IS FILLED WITH DIVINE LOVE, AND DIVINE LOVE WILL WORK ANY MIRACLE THAT NEEDS WORKING."

At regular periods and many, many times in between, while sitting or lying down, she mentally and audibly affirmed these words. She also made it a daily practice to send love thoughts to her family, friends, neighbors. She deliberately sent love thoughts to every person who had ever wronged her, or whom she had hurt or disliked. She searched her heart and mind to discover any hidden or long-forgotten wrongs or re-

_____

3. Published by Unity School of Christianity, Unity Village, MO 64065.

sentments. She forgave all, sending out love to every nationality, race, and creed. Often she declared: "THE CHRIST IN ME FORGIVES AND SENDS LOVE TO YOU."

A few weeks later the doubled fists began to loosen. Next, she could move one finger, then another. After a few months the pain ceased. Later she was able to use her hands perfectly, doing all her own work. This instance of healing occurred several years ago. Her doctor stated that the arthritis had probably been arrested forever.

The body has no initiative of its own. It is a living organism which the mind has built and continues to direct. This directive process is accomplished by means of mind impulses impinging on tissues sensitive to thought, which have been called brain cells. Brain cells have cores that receive and carry the thoughts and emotions of the presiding ego. Through the dynamic power of thought, man can release the life of the electrons secreted in the atoms that compose the cells of his body. By persistently dwelling upon the thought "divine love", man can change his beliefs and rebuild his body cell by cell. This lady proved it.

LOVE, A REQUIREMENT
IN PSYCHOSOMATIC TREATMENT

Some years ago, a doctor showed me a medical book on psychosomatic illness, which indicated the power of love for health and wholeness. In this book a group of doctors had compiled their analysis of various illnesses, and of the mental and emotional attitudes they felt caused these illnesses. I am amazed to see that in every analysis, the need for love was listed.

For instance, in the case of stomach disorders of all types, one of the psychosomatic reasons given for the illness was "love needed." In the case of heart disorders, one of the reasons listed was "love needed."

In the case of skin disorders, one of the reasons listed was "need for approval," which is a form of love. This brought to mind the experience a bookkeeper shared with me. She had had a skin disorder that defied healing, until she began daily placing her hands on her face, affirming: "DIVINE LOVE IS HEALING YOU NOW," and the skin disorder promptly began to heal.

In the case of female disorders, one of the reasons listed was "need for love." In the case of chronic fatigue, one of the psychosomatic reasons listed was "depression, insecurity and need for love."

In the case of the common headache and migraine, one of the reasons listed was "insecurity and need for love." I once talked with a businesswoman who was suffering from migraine headaches. Doctors had tried every type of medical treatment known in an effort to help her. She had also visited metaphysicians of various types trying to get freedom from those headaches.

When I asked, "Have you tried affirmative prayer as a possible means of healing your headaches?" she replied that affirmation was "too simple" a method to work for her. Several well-known spiritual healers in that area were mentioned, and I asked if she had contacted any of them for help. In each instance, she had. Then she proceeded to criticize them severely. Obviously, this woman needed to develop and generate a loving state of mind, if she was to be freed from her ill health. Her attitude bore witness to the psychosomatic findings of the doctors. This was pointed out to her and some affirmations on love were suggested for daily use.

In the case of excessive weight and over-eating, one of the reasons listed was "a feeling of dissatisfaction with life and a need for love." In the case of alcoholism and other excesses, one of the reasons listed was "feelings of inferiority and need for love."

Psychologists have long recognized the deprivation of love as a causative illness. Isn't it good to know that our medical doctors are now also realizing that whenever there is a health problem, there is a need for love?

It is good too, to realize that when there is such a need, *you can begin supplying it from within yourself.* As you radiate the love thought from within out, it is released into your mind, body, affairs and relationships; whatever outer forms of love are needed in your life are then attracted.

A businessman told me that he was healed of a painful condition of long standing after he began releasing love from within himself, by speaking words of love to his body. He had tried various treatments to no avail, and then he read the chapter showing how to generate love in my book, *The Dynamic Laws of Prosperity.*[4] He began placing his hands on the painful area of the body, saying over and over, "I love you." The pain gradually faded away.

POWERFUL THOUGHTS OF LOVE
THAT CAN HEAL

A powerful thought for healing is this: "God is love." If the full force of this statement were realized, a marvelous transformation would take place in man and his

---

4. Published by DeVorss & Company, Marina del Rey, CA. Rev. ed. 1985.

world. One person was healed of an incurable disease after he began daily affirming these words over and over.

In another instance, a lady sat by her sick husband's bed where he lay dying. Over and over she decreed: "God is love." Her husband rallied and made a complete recovery.

A man had been drinking for a number of days. He had visited ministers, a priest, a rabbi, and an assortment of social workers in an effort to terminate his drinking. Finally, he found his way to me.

Even though this man was still intoxicated at the time he arrived for help, he agreed to begin declaring affirmations with me just as soon as he could follow the words coherently. Meanwhile he agreed to sit quietly and accept the ideas expressed.

I began affirming to him over and over: "GOD LOVES YOU. GOD IS GUIDING YOU. GOD IS SHOWING YOU THE WAY." That God loved him was a new idea to this man, who had previously believed he was unloved and unwanted by the Deity because of his drinking. This thought, alone, was a sobering one.

Finally he joined me in affirming for himself: "GOD LOVES ME. GOD IS GUIDING ME. GOD IS SHOWING ME THE WAY." We continued this simple process of verbal affirmation for some time, until this man's mind cleared. At the conclusion of our prayer period, he walked out of my office a sober man.

On his way out, he mentioned that he had no place to go for the night; that along with the need for food and shelter, he also needed an overcoat to protect himself against the bitter cold weather. Knowing that this man had been the recipient of such items before, I felt it would strengthen his appreciation of them to attract these blessings through affirmation.

It was explained that his own use of words could continue to bless, guide, heal and provide for him. He agreed to momently affirm: "GOD LOVES ME, GOD IS GUIDING ME, GOD IS SHOWING ME THE WAY," as he walked toward the center of the city.

An old acquaintance drove by, recognized the man on foot, and offered him a ride into town. That very evening the friend presented him with a worn but warm overcoat, and gave him food and shelter until he found work.

A few weeks later, when this man returned to thank me, he appeared clean shaven, wearing fresh clothes. He had obtained work and was settled in his own rented room. As he began directing his thoughts and his life along constructive lines, he was able to make a complete comeback from a previous life of dissipation.

Many persons, as a result of being forced or suppressed in childhood, have hard, unyielding places in the subconscious mind, that do not readily yield to the power of the word. The word "love" overcomes those hard thoughts, which have caused mental and physical anguish. Since love is a harmonizing, constructive power, when it is made active in the mind of man, love conserves his substance. It reconstructs, rebuilds, and restores man and his world. This former "drunk" proved love's healing power.

A nurse, who had been working the night shift, was suffering from insomnia. Finally she visited her minister, explaining her inability to relax and sleep during the day, and her hesitancy to take habit-forming drugs for that purpose. The minister, explaining the healing effect of words on the body, asked the nurse to sit quietly in a big comfortable chair. Together they affirmed over and over: "I REST AND RELAX IN THE LOVE OF GOD, AND I AM HEALED."

It soon became apparent that the nurse was dozing, as the minister quietly continued affirming for her: "YOU REST AND RELAX IN THE LOVE OF GOD, AND YOU ARE HEALED." Soon she was fast asleep, snoring! Upon returning home, the nurse slept well for the first time in weeks. Her insomnia was gone.

A PRAYER GROUP'S FINDINGS ON LOVE

I know of a group of people who once experimented with the power of love in a prayer group, and found it to be the greatest thing in the world for solving both personal and business problems. Once a week these people met for an hour, and together affirmed statements on divine love. They brought to this prayer group their private prayer lists containing names of people and situations they wished to bless. No one else saw these prayer lists nor were the people and problems on these lists mentioned.

Instead, each person quietly placed his hands on his own list while the group affirmed together various statements on divine love: "DIVINE LOVE IS DOING ITS PERFECT WORK IN ME AND THROUGH ME NOW," they affirmed for themselves, for their own health, prosperity and happiness. "DIVINE LOVE IS DOING ITS PERFECT WORK IN YOU AND THROUGH YOU NOW," they affirmed for others.

In a quiet, peaceful way amazing things began to happen to the various members of that prayer group and to the people for whom they prayed. One businesswoman was out of harmony with a number of her friends. As she began dwelling on affirmations of love, these people began appearing unexpectedly at this prayer group, and reconciliation quickly took place.

Another businesswoman had been troubled for some time because of a misunderstanding that had arisen months previously between her and some friends. She had made every effort to apologize and bring about harmony again, but she had been coldly rebuffed through her letters, telephone calls and personal attempts.

One night, during the prayer time, as the group affirmed divine love for the names on their prayer lists, this woman and one other heard a tremendous popping noise in the air. One of the ladies discounted it, thinking it was the product of her imagination. But after the group had concluded, the second lady came to her and confidentially said, "Did you hear that popping sound in the air? That wasn't your imagination. It really happened! That was the hard thoughts that have existed between me and my friends being broken up. I am convinced that through our spoken words here tonight, divine love dissolved the inharmony that has existed."

From that night on, this lady had a completely different feeling about the previous inharmony, and quietly gave thanks that divine love had healed the situation. It proved to be so. Some weeks later, she felt led to contact her friends again. Instead of rebuffing her, this time they reacted as though nothing had ever been wrong between them. The previous cordiality was reestablished and continues still.

Divine love is the force that dissolves all opposers of true thought, and thus smooths out every obstacle that presents itself. When the substance of divine love is poured out upon alien thoughts, you are not bothered by them any more. When love harmonizes the consciousness, you find that your outer affairs are put in order too, and where once there was opposition and fear, cooperation and trust prevail.

A BUSINESSMAN'S SUCCESS FORMULA

Several years ago, a businessman related how he had developed his own private formula for "straightening out" troublesome people. He found that just by getting quiet and blessing them with an affirmation on love, it was as though an electrical force was generated, to which they became attuned. Usually, they quickly responded with harmonious attitudes and behavior. If not, further affirmations on love invariably produced satisfactory results.

Among his favorite love affirmations were these: "DIVINE LOVE BRINGS INTO MY LIFE THE RIGHT PEOPLE WHO CAN HELP ME AND MAKE ME HAPPY, AND WHOM I CAN HELP AND MAKE HAPPY. THOSE PEOPLE WHO ARE NOT FOR MY HIGHEST GOOD NOW FADE OUT OF MY LIFE, AND FIND THEIR GOOD ELSEWHERE. I WALK IN THE CHARMED CIRCLE OF GOD'S LOVE, AND I AM DIVINELY IRRESISTIBLE TO MY GREATEST GOOD NOW."

For troublesome people he affirmed: "I BEHOLD YOU WITH THE EYES OF LOVE, AND I GLORY IN YOUR PERFECTION NOW."

Ill health is often the result of inharmony in the home or office, which a person does not know how to throw off. The foregoing affirmations have a neutralizing, harmonizing effect on such situations and should be used daily for that purpose. *Disease is usually caused by a mind not at ease.* A famous surgeon recently pointed out that one of the requirements for good health is "harmony with people."

When you are inclined to wonder how just expressing thoughts and words of love can do much good in resolving your various problems, remind yourself that loving words and loving thoughts are super-charged with power to produce harmonious results. Indeed, it is the mission of love, both personally and impersonally, to produce wholeness in your life. Your job is not to wonder how love works, but to dare to release it from *within* yourself. As you do, you can witness interesting, satisfying, healing results.

THE MIRACLE LAW
OF HEALING

— Chapter 8 —

Everyone who reads the Bible knows about the healing power that Jesus Christ and His followers used centuries ago. The four Gospels and the Book of Acts are filled with healing accounts. What most people do not realize is that this same healing power is in our midst today, and is available to all of us. When invoked, it often produces results so amazing that we regard them as miracles.

Scientists tell us there are no miracles—only the working of higher laws not commonly understood. Actually there seems to be one set of natural laws for the physical world and another set for the invisible world of mind and spirit. *The laws of mind and spirit are so much stronger that they can be used to neutralize and even reverse the laws of the physical world, when necessary.* Jesus knew the higher laws of mind and spirit

132

and used them often to neutralize disease and produce apparent miracles. Developing the Christ-consciousness can give you access to that same miracle power!

HEALING OF A RUSSIAN IMMIGRANT

That the healing power of Jesus Christ is still mightily in our midst was first brought to my attention by an immigrant from Russia. In the 1920s he and his family, who had been politically and financially prominent in Russia, were suddenly banished to a concentration camp in Siberia. There they suffered all the horrors we have heard about in more recent times. As a result of ill treatment, his family died.

This man was daily beaten and expected to die, too. One night, nearly dead, he suddenly remembered something that a Christian missionary in the camp had suggested: When he needed a miracle, he could get it by calling upon the Name "Jesus Christ" for help.

As he lay in his cell in a semi-conscious state, he began to think about this Name and to call upon it. Suddenly the living presence of Jesus Christ appeared to him and asked his wishes. This dying man stated that he desired to be healed and freed from the concentration camp; if possible, he also wished to get to America to live and work.

Miraculously, it all happened. Even though he had been on his deathbed, he began to recover. New strength welled up within him, so that he was able to get up and move about in his cell the next day. Previously cruel guards lost interest in punishing him further. Through an amazing series of events, he was able to escape with several others from the camp, get out of Siberia into Europe, and eventually reach America, where he spent the rest of his life. At the time I met him, he showed me the severe scars he still bore—all a vivid reminder of the healing power that Jesus Christ still has.

THE SECRET OF COLOSSAL ACHIEVEMENT

No person's name has ever stood for such colossal achievement as the Name "Jesus Christ." There is still power for colossal achievement along all lines to those who dwell upon this Name today.

A woman saw her family going through great tribulation. Though she had prayed earnestly for them, their negative experience had continued. Finally she could think of no words to use for their deliverance, except the words "Jesus Christ." As she began to speak these words over and over, the tide turned, and her family came through their difficulties to safety.

Through repeated affirmations of the Name "Jesus Christ," a housewife undid much mischief and remade her home life, which had fallen into great distress and discord. The most harmonious relationships and environment were established as she persisted in calling upon this Name.

Repetition is the mother of wisdom. There is nothing that will benefit you like the continual repetition of the words "Jesus Christ." The followers of Jesus proved this. After His resurrection, the disciples gathered in an upper room in Jerusalem and dwelled upon His Name for approximately seven weeks. In the process, they were transformed from common, ignorant disciples into bold, illumined apostles of the early Christian era. Through dwelling upon His Name, this handful of ordinary men were able to spread the extraordinary message of Christianity to the whole ancient world — a colossal achievement for those times.

Charles Fillmore has described the power of dwelling upon the presence of the living Christ:

> Those who have for even a short time given their thoughts to the Christ Spirit can testify that it has developed in them a new outlook on life. Where before they were doubtful and uncertain, they now have the assurance of a power that is helping them to better living in every way. Health and prosperity have replaced the former fear of sickness and financial worry.[1]

HOW AN "INCURABLE" WAS HEALED

Speaking the Name "Jesus Christ" sets up a mighty vibration that releases miracle power. In this Name is the power to awaken the life, substance and intelligence that lies within every cell of your body. In the Name "Jesus Christ" is the power to mold universal substance as supply, peace, harmony or guidance. *When spoken, this Name sets into activity forces that produce miraculous results.*

One of the spiritual counselors who worked with Myrtle Fillmore in the early days of the Unity movement once explained how so many miraculous healings took place — through dwelling upon the Name "Jesus Christ." Mrs. Fillmore literally "drilled" her prayer workers in the healing consciousness of Jesus Christ. Over and

---

1. Fillmore, *Keep a True Lent*, (Unity Village, MO 64065: Unity Books, 1953) pp. 28-29.

over they affirmed His presence and power in their midst, as they sought healing for the many who turned to them. As each worker developed a healing consciousness, he then counseled with those who appeared for help.

This counselor spoke of the time she had spent the day riding street cars, making hospital and house calls on the sick in Kansas City. Arriving back at the Unity headquarters late in the afternoon, she was tired and anxious to get home. But there she found waiting for her a woman who had been told she had an incurable disease with only a short time to live. This fearful woman desired prayers for her condition. No one else was available to pray with her, and the tired counselor thought, "How can I possibly pray for this woman's health just now, when I am so fatigued myself?"

Nevertheless, they sat down together and quietly relaxed into prayer. For some time the counselor silently meditated upon the Name "Jesus Christ." As she did, a feeling of life-strength, vitality flowed into her being, followed by a feeling of peace that assured her of worthwhile results. A half hour or so later, when she concluded her meditation period, the one seeking help said "Jesus Christ was here. I saw Him in our midst while you prayed. And I felt a change take place in my body. I have been healed." The coming days proved her words to be true. In that quiet hour a permanent healing had occurred.

By declaring and decreeing the Name "Jesus Christ" you send into the body a spiritual force that shatters fixed states of mind that have caused disease. Mental prisons are opened, and your imprisoned thoughts and emotions go free to produce new health.

CANCER HEALED

There is a marvelous power for protection and deliverance in this Name when it is earnestly spoken or even silently recognized.

Charles Fillmore has promised:

> Whoever you are, wherever you are, Jesus in His spiritual consciousness is waiting for your mental recognition. Whatever your object, He will show you how to attain it. "Whatsoever ye shall ask in My Name, that will I do!"[2]

A housewife was in the hospital, having been operated on the second time for cancer. She was not expected to live. Several members of her family had died of cancer, and it was assumed that she would, too.

One night when she was very weak and not expected to get through the night, she realized that the angel of death was standing on the left side of her bed, waiting for her. "If I can just make it until morning, I may live, but if I have to exert myself even so much as to cough, I will be gone," she mused.

Suddenly she remembered having heard of the vitalizing power that is in the Name "Jesus Christ." Weakly she began to meditate upon that Name. After a while, it was as though a great light came into the room and stood near her bed, on the right side. In the midst of this great light, appeared the figure of Jesus Christ. When the dying woman saw Him and felt His presence, a great sense of peace and relief descended upon her. The angel of death quietly withdrew. No

---

2. *Keep a True Lent*, p. 164.

longer afraid, she relaxed into a deep sleep. Upon waking the next morning, she was filled with vitality. A deep feeling of joy permeated her whole being, and she knew she would live. It was a glorious feeling.

That was several decades ago. This woman completely recovered and found that a complete healing had taken place, not only in her body, but also in her personality. Whereas she had previously been a whinning complainer who had made life miserable for her husband and family, she now began to count her blessings. Feeling that her life had been spared for some constructive reason, she took up the study of Truth and became active in her church. There she served as a channel of inspiration and healing to many others.

HOW TO TAP THE POWER

There was a tremendous power ready to burst forth in the Name of Jesus Christ twenty centuries ago. That power still exists today. The Name "Jesus Christ" is like an alabaster box that has to be sharply broken open, before the precious ointment may pour forth as healing power. You should not be discouraged if your first attempts at calling on the Name "Jesus Christ" do not bring the results you desire. *It is in the repeated declarations of this Name that its power is released.*

As you persist in affirming this Name, you can be assured that the term "Jesus Christ" holds all power within it, and is worth working with, until that power has been tapped. Jesus Christ tried to impress upon His disciples that there is power in His Name to accomplish all things. *When speaking the Name "Jesus*

Christ," do so with authority; you then set in motion a mighty force to accomplish results. Take the Name "Jesus Christ" and affirm it often. There is surely power in it that opens ways to your good which the finite mind never dreamed of.

When you repeat this Name often, you come into possession of whatever knowledge or power you need to meet any given situation victoriously. As you dwell upon the Name "Jesus Christ," you will find yourself knowing all you need to know, as you need to know it. New life and energy will come alive in your body. New peace and harmony will come alive in your affairs. New substance will come alive in your financial matters. Indeed, your mind will be renewed, and your body and affairs transformed. Old things will pass away. New good will come so that it may even seem you have been reborn.

One of my first experiences in witnessing the healing power of the Christ consciousness came when an ailing woman telephoned for prayers. This lady was constantly in need of healing. As soon as one ailment was cured, another appeared. This woman obviously "enjoyed" ill health and subconsciously invited it. She craved the attention received through being sick, and her illnesses were actually self-inflicted. However, when the pain became sufficiently uncomfortable, she always wanted relief.

One afternoon as she telephoned for prayers, I was busily dictating to my secretary. My first reaction to her request for prayer was, "How shall I pray so that this woman will be permanently healed? I have worn out every prayer I know trying to help her." In a flash the thought came, "Stop trying to heal her. Cast the burden of her healing on the living Christ."

Immediately I asked my secretary to join me in a prayer for the caller. Together we relaxed, became quiet, and affirmed: "I CAST THIS BURDEN OF HEALING ON JESUS CHRIST. JESUS CHRIST IS HERE, HEALING, HEAL-ING, HEALING." A little later we affirmed: "CHRIST IN YOU NOW FREES YOU FROM ALL LIMITATION. YOU ARE UN-FETTERED AND UNBOUND. YOU ARE NOW HEALED IN THE NAME OF JESUS CHRIST, AND YOU MENTALLY ACCEPT YOUR PERMANENT HEALING NOW." When a sense of peace and release came, we terminated our prayer time and went back to work.

Within the hour this lady telephoned again to say all pain was gone. Thereafter her calls for healing became fewer and fewer, which indicated she had, at last, begun to mentally accept healing.

A MIRACLE FORMULA

One of the great metaphysical healers at the turn of the twentieth century was Emma Curtis Hopkins, who ministered to more than fifty thousand people, in the days before the mass media of radio and television. In her book, *Scientific Christian Mental Practice*, she has promised:

> Looking mentally upon Jesus Christ as present will cure poverty, deafness, blindness, palsy, rheumatism, insanity. Since He has never left us, we can look upon Him mentally and be cured of whatever ailment we cry about.[3]

---

3. Published by DeVorss & Company, Marina del Rey, CA 90294.

Why is the practice of looking mentally upon Jesus Christ as present so powerful a formula for healing? Because through His great overcoming for all mankind, *Jesus Christ broke through the negative thought strata into which the race had fallen. By breaking through these negative thought strata, He opened the way for all who become attuned to His power, to do likewise.*

If you desire to demonstrate over problems that no amount of prayer, spiritual study, medical treatment, psychiatric attention or just plain hard work have been able to overcome—then begin dwelling upon the Name "Jesus Christ," asking His help. *As you daily affirm His Name and call on his power, you will make a "major breakthrough" out of the negative thought strata that have bound you, into higher levels of consciousness. There you will be free to claim your good.*

In some instances you will actually know when you "crash through" the negative thought strata that previously bound you. At other times, you will simply feel uplifted above all former difficulties. As you "come up over" them (which is the way to "overcome" them), they will fade away and you will find that so-called miracles have taken place.

Especially powerful prayers for breaking through negation to your good are these:

1. THERE IS NOTHING IN ALL THE WORLD FOR ME TO FEAR, FOR GREATER IS THE MIRACLE-WORKING POWER OF JESUS CHRIST HERE AND NOW THAN ANY OTHER APPEARANCE.

2. OF MYSELF I CANNOT DO IT, BUT JESUS CHRIST CAN AND IS PERFORMING MIRACLES IN MY MIND, BODY, AND AFFAIRS HERE AND NOW.

3. THE MIRACLE-WORKING POWER OF JESUS CHRIST IS ACTIVELY AT WORK IN MY MIND, BODY, AND AFFAIRS NOW, AND THEY ARE EVERY WHIT WHOLE.

4. THE MIRACLE-WORKING POWER OF JESUS CHRIST IS NOW RELEASED INTO THIS APPEARANCE (SITUATION, PERSONALITY, DIAGNOSIS), AND HIS PERFECT RESULTS NOW MANIFEST.

5. I CAST THIS BURDEN ON JESUS CHRIST AND I GO FREE NOW TO RECEIVE MY SUPREME GOOD.

WHAT THE CHRIST CONSCIOUSNESS CAN DO

In 1923 the first "healing rally" was held at the Unity headquarters in Kansas City, to which people came from all over the country. It was a two-weeks affair. At the close of this conference, those who had received healings during the meetings were asked to rise. More than nine-tenths of the audience stood up!

Later some of the healing testimonials appeared in *Unity*[4] magazine. A lady who had worn glasses most of her life received a healing of her sight, and removed her glasses. Another woman was healed of cancer of the breast, after her physicians had operated for the last time. A businessman was healed of asthma. Another was healed of the intense pain that had resulted from decaying bones between his shoulders. A thin, emaciated woman who had been literally carried into the conference unable to walk, began gaining weight and was able to walk about freely before the meetings were over.

---

4. Published by Unity School of Christianity, Unity Village MO 64065.

What produced these and many other healings?
During the conference, Charles Fillmore talked a lot about the living presence and power of Jesus Christ. In one talk he said:

> We have no human leader of the Unity movement. There is only one head, Jesus Christ. "But," you say, "Jesus Christ is gone." I assure you that He has not gone. He is in our midst today. He has been seen again and again standing on this platform. "Where two or three are gathered together in my name, there am I in the midst of them." We are here gathered together in the Name of Jesus Christ. Jesus is here in his personal body, raised to the fourth dimension. Jesus is here in His glorified body. As John saw him on the Island of Patmos, so many are seeing him in this day. A number of persons have testified to seeing Him in this chapel, and we believe their testimony. We see him and feel him and also have the assurance of His presence and guidance through all avenues.

A growing number of non-denominational ministers are healing mankind in the Name of Jesus Christ all over the world. I once talked with one such minister who is noted for his Christ consciousness which has healed countless people of all types of disease, including the well-known list of "incurables."

When I inquired into this minister's healing methods, he said, "It is simple. I just call on the presence and power of Jesus Christ to heal. He does the work. He is as much in our midst now as He was two thousand years ago. The Master will lovingly respond to anyone who turns to Him for help." He then related several recent healings of cancer among his congregation that had taken place after he had begun calling on Jesus Christ to heal.

HOW MAJOR AND MINOR HEALINGS OCCURRED

In minor, as well as major healing needs, the Jesus Christ consciousness has power. A domestic worker hurried down the steps of her home to attend a lecture on healing. In her haste, she fell, cutting her forehead near the eye, causing pain and swelling in one shoulder, arm and hand. A relative, witnessing her mishap said, "You must go to bed at once and let me telephone for a doctor. You are seriously hurt." But this little lady was determined to hear the lecture. Ignoring this warning, she painfully proceeded on her way.

At the close of the lecture she approached the speaker, obviously in pain. The cut near her eye had continued to bleed and her fingers, arm and shoulder were badly swollen. Realizing this, the lecturer quickly declared, "You are now healed in the Name of Jesus Christ!" The lady humbly repeated these words aloud, "Yes, I am now healed in the Name of Jesus Christ!" As these words were spoken all "misery" left her body. Though it took several days for the swelling to disappear and for the cut to mend, a healing had taken place. *The Name "Jesus Christ" holds all power within it, which is released through the spoken word.* This lady proved it.

A businessman found that the best way to enter into periods of deep meditation was by first affirming over and over the Name "Jesus Christ." One night, during a meditation, he prayed for the healing of three friends who were in the hospital seriously ill. In his prayer period he pictured Jesus Christ healing those friends. As he did, he "saw" the three friends following Jesus Christ out of the hospital. This flash assured him that they would be all right. All three soon were released from the hospital on the same day!

An elderly woman was supposed to go on a vacation tour. But only a few days before the trip, she "came down" with lumbago. In bed, unable to walk, she refused to give up to her illness as she repeatedly affirmed: "JESUS CHRIST IS HERE, HEALING ME NOW. WITH HIS HELP, I SHALL RISE AND WALK." For several days her prayers seemed in vain, as the pain continued. But she persisted in affirmation.

At two o'clock A.M. on the morning she was scheduled to leave on her trip, she awakened to realize that all pain was gone; her body was filled with energy. She *did* arise from her bed and walk. As she and her husband joined the tour they were shown America's largest cave. In fact, this lady out-walked her healthy husband, who decided to bypass the last phase of this walking tour.

PARALYSIS, RHEUMATISM, HEART TROUBLE HEALED

A businessman was suffering from a painful condition of paralysis, which persisted in spite of the finest medical care. After studying the healings of Jesus as recorded in the New Testament, he began daily affirming: "THE HEALING POWER OF JESUS CHRIST SURGES THROUGH ME, RAISING ME UP TO PERFECT HEALTH."

Almost immediately signs of recuperation became evident: first, there was a freedom from pain; then he was able to take slow but steady steps from his room; next, he walked in his garden. In a few short months he manifested perfect health. As this man discovered, you may look for wonderful things to occur when you affirm the Name "Jesus Christ." You may even expect the impossible!

Another businessman was in considerable pain from rheumatism, which doctors had been unable to relieve. He also had a bad heart which had troubled him since early manhood. Medical specialists had predicted that he would soon become a complete invalid.

Not wishing to accept such a diagnosis, this man kept searching for healing. Upon learning of the healing power to be found in the Christ consciousness, he repeated thousands of times a prayer given him by a friend: "CHRIST IN ME RENEWS MY MIND AND BODY. CHRIST IN ME NOW RESTORES ME TO WHOLENESS AND HEALTH."

Within a month, the rheumatism was much better. Within six weeks the pain was gone, except for an occasional twinge which later disappeared. As for his heart condition, he soon threw away the digitalis and quinine, which he had taken for years.

When later health problems appeared, the same healing technique produced healthy results: A bad case of bleeding gums, an attack of pneumonia, and a hernia completely disappeared as the healing power of Jesus Christ was affirmed.

Later, in reviewing these experiences, this man stated:

"Perhaps the greatest change brought about by these healings has been the change within myself. I am a man well into middle age who would be accounted extremely sophisticated. Once a complete agnostic, I now accept without question the healing power of Jesus Christ. Through my own experiences, I have been able to bring a number of people closer to the healing power that can still be found in practical Christianity."

HOW TO CAUSE AFFAIRS AND EVENTS
TO MOVE WITH EASE

Right in the midst of the most desperate situations, begin to dwell upon the power of Jesus Christ to help you. That will be the first mental move in dissolving the darkness. Calling on the Name "Jesus Christ" can cause affairs and events to move with ease.

You can invoke the miracle power of Jesus Christ in several simple ways:

First: By deliberately turning your attention toward Him and asking His help.

Second: By repeatedly speaking the Name "Jesus Christ."

Third: By repeatedly meditating upon the Name "Jesus Christ," letting it reveal its presence, power and guidance to you.

Fourth: By repeatedly picturing Jesus Christ amid any situation, condition or personality that distresses you, producing perfect results.

THE SUCCESS POWER OF A SECRET TEXT

Those who have triumphed over difficult experiences have often had a secret word, motto or text which they held to in time of trial. This secret text rearranged their affairs, bringing them through to victory. The mystics of old felt that the Name "Jesus Christ" was such a text; for any troublesome situation, they would affirm: "Come, Jesus Christ."

A secretary once proved the power of using this secret text. The firm for which she worked had hired a manager who appeared totally incapable. Within a few months, financial difficulties and personality clashes within the firm had arisen. Yet those who had hired this man did not realize he was the cause of their sudden troubles. This man cleverly concealed his true attitudes and methods.

After a particularly hectic day, this secretary remained on in the office after the others had gone. As she walked the floor she affirmed: "JESUS CHRIST IS HERE PRODUCING PERFECT RESULTS." Hundreds of times she declared this statement, until she felt the turmoil and burden of the situation pass. Her secret text had done its perfect work. Within a matter of days, the incapable manager resigned. When he left, so did the previous confusion which he had caused.

There has long been a belief in the religious world that there is somewhere a "lost word of power" which, when found and uttered, will set all things right. The Hebrews felt that this "lost word" was once known to their priesthood. When correctly used, it had brought miraculous results instantly. The early Christians felt that this "lost word of power" was to be found in the continual repetition of the Name "Jesus Christ."

Make this Name your secret text, your miracle text!

THE OCCULT LAW
OF HEALING

— Chapter 9 —

When life seems full of defeats, discouragements and dangers, that is the time to invoke the occult law of healing. You can do it by looking away from the discouraging experiences and affirming often two special, power-packed words: "*I AM.*"

The word "occult" means that which is secret. The ancient Egyptians had a special secret name they called on for producing wonderful results. That occult name was "*I AM.*"

The young prince Moses learned the secret power that could be released through that name at the court of Pharaoh. That the Egyptians placed great power in this name was evident to Moses, since the words "*I AM*" appeared upon the walls of every Egyptian temple built at that time.

When Jehovah instructed Moses to use this all-powerful name to rescue the Hebrews from the dreaded Pharaoh, Moses knew that extraordinary power would accompany him on his mission. As he invoked that "*I AM*" power, he not only rescued the future Hebrew nation from cruel slavery, but he also performed the amazing tasks of feeding them for forty years in the barren wilderness; of healing his critical sister of leprosy; and of making the Hebrews' dream come true as he led them to the border of their longed-for promised land.

At the close of his life, Moses reminded the Hebrews of further feats: In all those dreary wilderness years, their clothes or shoes had not "waxed old" upon them. At the age of one hundred and twenty, in spite of all he had been through, Moses' eyes were not dim nor his natural forces abated. (Deuteronomy 34:7) When this incredible man died, his accomplishments (any of which was an amazing feat) included: Emancipator of the Hebrews; prophet of God; architect of moral law and order; founder of the Hebrew nation; warrior; legislator; judge; priest; organizer and miracle worker.[1]

MOSES' SECRET TEXT FOR SUCCESS CAN BE YOURS

"*I AM*" was the Hebrews' name for God, for good, and they became known as "People of the *I AM*." This occult term "*I AM*," has often been described as the "song of Moses," because it was his secret text for success. It can be yours.

---

1. See the author's book, *The Millionaire Moses.*

*There are strange powers lying dormant within that
name. All that you dream of as desirable can be released through the redeeming words, "I AM," because
these words stir up the divine nature within you. "I
AM" is the name of God within you.* Jesus made refer-
ence to it as the kingdom of God within man. (Luke
17:21) To meditate consistently on the statement, "I
AM THE LIGHT OF MY WORLD," can flood your whole being with light and drive out all darkness. Scientists tell
us that at the center of every cell and atom of the body
is light. When that light is recognized and turned on
by the mind of man, the dark appearance of disease,
depression, confusion and inharmony flee.

THE REDEEMING POWER OF THIS NAME

Many years ago during one of the Midwest's most
severe winters, a young boy learned the redeeming
power that is released through this name.

He had lost his job. Without work, his financial supply was gone. Having gotten behind with his rent, the
landlady shut off the heat in his room. With no money
to buy food, he became hungry and weak. From his
point of view, there seemed no solution to his plight.

Far into the night this young man pondered his di-
lemma and tried to find a solution. Finally he decided
that the only solution was to go down to the Missouri
River, jump in and end it all.

In the wee small hours of that stormy morning, he
started his cold, hungry march to the river. On this
uncomfortable journey, he sought temporary shelter
from the icy winds by huddling in a store doorway.
There he hoped to gain strength and warmth enough

to resume his walk. As he huddled there, his head began to whirl. Still conscious, but weak, he suddenly heard a voice say, *"I AM."* Startled, he assumed some- one had followed him. But there was no one near in that black, cold night. Concluding it must be his own imagination, he again huddled. And again his head began to whirl, as he heard the same voice say a second time, *"I AM."* This time, though, he realized the voice came from deep *within* himself.

Puzzled at what it meant, he began repeating the words he had heard over and over: *"I AM, I AM, I AM."* A strange fascination for those words grew within him. As he continued contemplating their meaning, he soon realized that his body was getting warm with a glow of new life. Continued affirmation of these words caused him to realize that his hunger had disappeared and his mind was strangely clear. A new strength had entered both mind and body.

Again the boy stepped out into the street, but this time he walked back toward his room, away from the icy river. On his way, he continued repeating these mysterious but powerful words, *"I AM."* Upon opening the door to his previously cold, damp room, he real- ized it now was warm, though the heat had not been turned on. In mystical comfort, he went to bed and slept soundly.

The next morning he hurriedly dressed, and follow- ing a strong hunch, revisited one of the businesses where he had been refused work only the day before. This time, the man in charge unquestioningly assigned him to a job at a good salary. With this happy turn of events, previously impossible problems began to dis- solve. This young man continued making the words *"I AM"* his secret text and his life became one of increasing success. The "song of Moses" had become his song. Use of the words *"I AM"* can surely give you something to sing about, too!

HOW TO USE THIS OCCULT POWER TO PRODUCE ASTONISHING RESULTS

Just as the Hebrews of old, we are all "people of the *I AM*." When you go forth using the name *"I AM"* in a positive, uplifting way, it opens every door for you. It dissolves every obstacle. It prepares the way to your good, and then leads you to it. As this young man discovered, every time you say, think, or feel the words *"I AM"*, you have gripped a handle of power. *Every time you say "I AM", you have released a dynamic force that is going to produce results.*

Since this dynamic force has no choice but to produce whatever you join to it, be careful what you attach to the words *"I AM."* If you say, "I am sick," "I am tired," "I am weak," "I am getting old," "I am unhappy," "I am lonely," "I am a failure," "I am discouraged," you are exercising a power that will produce those results.

Even though it doesn't seem true at the moment, if you say, "I am healthy," "I am happy," "I am prosperous," "I am a success," it will begin to come true. Jesus apparently knew the tremendous power that can be released in these words, because he often used *"I AM"* statements upward:

I *am* the way, the truth and the life. (John 14:6)

I *am* the resurrection and the life. (John 11:25)

I am the bread of life. (John 6:48)

I am a king. (John 18:37)

I am the good shepherd. (John 10:11)

Before Abraham was born, *I am.* (John 8:58)

Does it sound foolish to you that *"I AM"* spoken upward toward the good is sure to outpicture that good as success, health, happiness? Do you doubt that such power is released through speaking that name?

If so, try an experiment: Just go into a room alone, close your eyes, and turn your attention within, saying over and over the words, *"I AM."* Soon you will find your whole being filled with a sense of power which you never felt before — power to overcome, to accomplish, to stir up health and vitality; power to do all that needs to be done by you. *Just try for one week always saying the words "I AM" upward, toward the good. You will be astonished at the results!*

FORMULA FOR HEALING, SUCCESS AND JOY

Your *"I AM"* power is especially effective in healing. *When you speak the words "I AM", every cell and atom of your being springs to attention!* Realizing this, the prophet Joel advised: "Let the weak say, '*I am* strong.'" (Joel 3:10)

Many people have experienced healings of mind, body and affairs by using the following simple formula:

On retiring at night, just before going to sleep, repeat either mentally or verbally:

I AM HEALTH, STRENGTH, PEACE, HAPPINESS, AND PROS-
PERITY.

THE SPIRIT OF GOD, WHICH IS ACTIVE IN ME, FLOWS
THROUGH MY PHYSICAL BODY, IN A PURIFYING, CLEANS-
ING, HEALING STREAM THAT REMOVES ALL OBSTRUCTIONS
AND BRINGS PEACE, HEALTH, AND HARMONY TO MY BODY.

I AM WELL, STRONG, VITAL.

I AM BEAUTIFUL, PEACEFUL, POISED.

I AM ETERNALLY YOUTHFUL.

I AM BUOYANT, HAPPY, FREE.

I SHALL ARISE IN THE MORNING FILLED WITH ENERGY,
RADIANCE, AND THE POWER TO ACCOMPLISH WHATEVER I
FIND TO DO.

Others have worked out their problems, from overcoming poverty to healing physical disorders by this
simple process. So can you!

Does this simple formula sound too good to be true?
If you doubt its power, then reverse the process. Try
saying over and over, "I am a failure. I am, I am,
I am!" See how terrible you will soon feel, and how dis-
orderly your affairs will become; whereas if you insist,
"I am a success," you can watch the events of your life
begin to move in that direction.

A secretary, upon learning of this *"I AM"* power,
decided to test its effect in her office, where her fellow
workers had been unhappy and unpleasant about
many things. As she silently affirmed, *"I am joy"*,
amid the gloom, her fellow workers became so joyous
that within a few days she had to give up her experiment. The hilarity was beginning to disrupt their work
and interfere with the office schedule!

HOW TO SURMOUNT ALL DIFFICULTIES

A lady with chronic health problems talked incessantly about her troubles. She was also a chronic complainer. Upon learning of the occult law of healing, she realized she had been using her *"I AM"* power downward, toward disease and lack, and had reaped corresponding results.

One day she resolved to "change her tune" and began saying, "I am going to make it," meaning: "I am going to get well and solve all my problems." That was the turning point in her health and in her life. As she continued affirming *"I AM"* statements upward toward the good, her chronic problems faded away.

You make your destiny by the things which you attach to the words "I AM." If you say, "I am afraid," you destroy yourself through fear. If you say, "I am one with God and His goodness," you immediately begin to improve your life.

Emmet Fox once advised: "Say to your problems, *'I AM* hath sent me,' and the way will open for you to surmount all difficulties."[2]

A housewife had a toothache which she had been unable to overcome. Finally, remembering the occult law of healing, she began affirming *"I AM"* upward: "I AM THE RADIANT CHILD OF GOD, I AM, I AM, I AM." The pain faded and the swelling subsided.

A grandmother watched the fever and infection leave her grandchild, while holding the child in her arms, as she affirmed: "I AM LIFE, I AM LIFE, I AM LIFE."

---

2. Emmet Fox, *The Ten Commandments* (New York: Harper & Row, 1953).

One metaphysician has predicted that the day will come when people in hospitals will stop saying, "I am sick," and will be healed by using their *"I AM"* powers upward. Of course, when people learn the preventive power in this name, they will no longer find ill health or hospitalization a part of their experience.

You can decree peace of mind and body by quietly decreeing, "I AM PEACE." The body is wonderfully obedient to the words *"I AM"* and hastens to do their bidding. When that bidding is upward toward the good, the body is renewed, even transformed. Jesus' decree, *"I AM* the resurrection and the life," is a powerful prayer for bodily renewal. Continual repetition of the words *"I AM"* sets the mind in order and the body at ease.

There once was a businessman who was supposed to be dying of an incurable disease. Hearing of the unlimited power to be found in the words *"I AM,"* he affirmed over and over, "PRAISE GOD, I AM HEALED," so long that it finally happened.

COLLEGE DEAN HEALED
OF NERVOUS BREAKDOWN

A dean of university women had suffered a nervous breakdown. For several months she was confined to the home of a relative, receiving constant medical care. Though her condition improved, her complete healing did not come.

One day her relative shared with her some inspirational literature. As she read it, her mind became calm, and for the first time she felt assured of a complete recovery.

Thereafter, in consultation with a minister, she was shown that the nature of God is good; that this God-nature was within her as her *"I AM"* power. It was suggested that she begin calling forth the health and wholeness of mind and body by using bold, deliberate *"I AM"* health statements.

Daily she affirmed: "I AM THE PERFECT CHILD OF GOD. I AM! I AM! I AM! I AM LETTING THE CHRIST MIND EXPRESS LIFE AND WHOLENESS THROUGH ME NOW. I AM! I AM! I AM! I AM WHOLE, WELL, PERFECT. I AM! I AM! I AM! MY MIND, BODY, AND AFFAIRS ARE NOW IN DIVINE ORDER. I AM HEALED, PRAISE GOD, I AM HEALED. I AM! I AM! I AM!"

At first, she hesitated to use such bold statements. But as she did so, even hesitantly at first, she began to feel calm, peaceful, and reassured about her health. Within a couple of weeks, she went back to her responsible, demanding university job, and she continued to use bold *"I AM"* affirmations for her health, guidance and success. Thereafter she enjoyed the best of health.

Often those people who accept their *"I AM"* power and use it in *"I AM"* affirmations, experience healings when nothing else has produced them. Somehow their *"I AM"* power, when recognized, dissolves the emotional and physical barriers that have held back restoration previously.

THE SUCCESS POWER OF THIS NAME

Not only did the Hebrews and the ancient Egyptians know there was great power in the name *"I AM,"* but other great civilizations of the past used these words as their secret text for success, too.

In the sixth century B.C., a man from ancient Iran name Zoroaster, began to daily meditate upon the words *"I AM."* Not only did he step out of the rank and file of common men into the rulership of his nation, but he also founded the prominent Persian religion, Zoroastrianism, which became the world's first universal religion.

Charles Fillmore once described the success power to be found when you make *"I AM"* your secret text:

> Every time you send out a thought of wholehearted faith in the *"I AM"* part of yourself, you set in motion a chain of causes that must bring the results you seek. Ask whatsoever you will in the name of the *"I AM,"* the divine within, and your demands will be fulfilled; both heaven and earth will hasten to do your bidding. The *"I AM"* consciousness will lead you out of the desert of negation and into the Promised Land of plenty that flows with milk and honey.[3]

There once was a young servant girl who proved the success power to be found in this name. She strongly desired to become a foreign missionary for a certain religious group, but she had not the required training. Nevertheless, she kept affirming: *"I am* going to be a missionary, because with God all things are possible."

As she kept using her *"I AM"* power upward, a group of delegates representing another denomination invited her to go abroad as one of their missionaries. They decided that her great desire and zeal to spread the Truth was far more important to their cause than any amount of education could be.

---

3. Fillmore, *Prosperity* (Unity Village, MO 64065: Unity Books) pp. 93, 98.

THE AUTHOR'S EXPERIENCES WITH
THE LOST WORD OF POWER

Early in my ministry, I decided to experiment in prayer with *"I AM"* statements, just to test their power. The results astounded me.

At that time, a member of my prayer ministry met with me each weekday morning at eleven o'clock in the church prayer room, for an hour of affirmative prayer and meditation. This prayer partner happened to be a very busy businessman, a member of the church board, who took an hour daily from the pressure of his work to pray with me about church business, the names in the prayer ministry, and other matters.

Realizing that the early Christians considered the Name "Jesus Christ" to be "the lost word of power," whereas the people of the Old Testament considered the name *"I AM"* to be the "lost word of power," it occurred to me that combining the two names might have special effectiveness.

For a number of months, among the other affirmations used, my prayer partner and I daily affirmed:

"I AM THE CHRIST MIND, I AM, I AM, I AM! I AM LETTING THE CHRIST MIND THINK TRUTH THROUGH ME, I AM, I AM, I AM! I AM LETTING THE CHRIST MIND REVEAL THE TRUTH TO ME, I AM, I AM, I AM! I AM LETTING THE CHRIST MIND EXPRESS THE TRUTH THROUGH ME, I AM, I AM, I AM!"

Placing our hands on our prayer lists, we affirmed:

"I AM LETTING THE CHRIST MIND HEAL THROUGH ME, I AM, I AM, I AM! I AM LETTING THE CHRIST MIND PROSPER THROUGH ME, I AM, I AM, I AM! I AM LETTING THE CHRIST MIND PRODUCE PERFECT RESULTS THROUGH ME, I AM, I AM, I AM!"

As we daily met and affirmed these words over and over quietly, we could feel a powerful presence in our midst. It was as though a cool breeze came into that prayer room—a healing balm, which might be described as the Holy Spirit, or as the whole spirit of good.

Continued affirmation caused a power deep within to awaken. A warm, soothing feeling of life then spiritually fed and renewed us; it also inspired us concerning anything we needed to know for our personal welfare and for the good of the church.

Through my use of these "I AM" affirmations, I found that my spiritual understanding increased considerably. People were healed just by attending classes and services at the church, and the lives of others vastly improved through receiving private counseling.

Amazing insight was given me into church matters that brought happy results in reorganization, redecoration, new members, and increased income. Also, it was as though a super-intelligence within me had been tapped, so that I wrote prolifically during that period.

The practical results that followed the practice of "I AM" affirmations for this businessman were these: His financial affairs prospered so during this period that he gave thousands of dollars in tithes to the church. He also received vast improvement in a health problem that had troubled him for years.

HOW TO USE THIS CREATIVE POWER OF THE UNIVERSE TO WHICH NOTHING IS IMPOSSIBLE!

We discovered that the "I AM" power within is a creative power.

Its business is to attend to your every call, and to bring into manifestation that which you decree through your spoken words. As you deliberately use your *"I AM"* power upward toward the good, you can walk free and independent of trouble and sorrow, untouched by it. You can walk the road of life triumphantly, gloriously, as the radiant, victorious child of God that you are.

Through proper use of your *"I AM"* power, you will find yourself filled with the creative power of the universe, to which nothing is impossible. As you dwell upon your *"I AM"* power, you will fulfill your divine destiny, experiencing peace, health, and plenty here and now.

For this purpose affirm often:

I AM ONE WITH GOD, I AM ONE WITH GOOD.

I AM THE RADIANT CHILD OF GOD, I AM,
    I AM, I AM!

I AM THE HEALTHY CHILD OF GOD, I AM,
    I AM, I AM!

I AM THE PROSPEROUS CHILD OF GOD, I AM,
    I AM, I AM!

I AM THE HAPPY CHILD OF GOD, I AM, I AM,
    I AM!

I AM THE ILLUMINED CHILD OF GOD, I AM,
    I AM, I AM!

I AM THE OVERCOMING CHILD OF GOD, I AM,
    I AM, I AM!

I AM THE VICTORIOUS CHILD OF GOD, I AM,
    I AM, I AM!

I AM THE SUCCESSFUL CHILD OF GOD, I AM,
I AM, I AM!

I AM THE LOVED AND BELOVED CHILD OF
GOD I AM, I AM, I AM!

I AM A PART OF THE CREATIVE POWER OF
THE UNIVERSE, TO WHICH NOTHING IS
IMPOSSIBLE. I AM, I AM, I AM!

I AM RICH, WELL AND HAPPY, AND ALL MY
AFFAIRS ARE NOW IN DIVINE ORDER.

THE IMAGING LAW
OF HEALING

— Chapter 10 —

A doctor of chiropractic first introduced me to the imaging law of healing, when he pointed out how often proper use of the imagination had helped to overcome serious health problems in his patients.

A distraught mother brought her daughter to him for treatment saying, "I really don't know why I keep trying to find a cure for my daughter's skin condition, since I know it is incurable."

This chiropractor asked, "What makes you think her skin condition is incurable?"

"Because every doctor that I have talked with has said so," retorted the mother.

The doctor replied, "That only means her condition is incurable *in their opinion*, but that does not mean her condition is incurable. *Nothing is incurable in*

God's sight. Scientists tell us that the body is constantly rebuilding and curing itself. When the body is fed the mental picture of wholeness, it builds its cells according to that picture; whereas when fed thoughts of hopelessness and incurability, the body builds the cells according to that mental picture."

In this way, he set up in the mother's mind a mental picture that her daughter could be healed. He then talked with the little girl, asking what she would most like to do when her skin was again clear. She replied that she wanted to go swimming. Taking some money from his wallet, the doctor said, "See this money? It will be yours for that swim the day you come for final treatment."

Each time she returned for a chiropractic adjustment, he spoke of the day she would be completely well again and would head for the swimming pool. In this way, the mental image of healing was stimulated and accepted.

It took a number of weeks of steady treatment and mental imagery, but this child's condition cleared up completely. On the day she came in for that final treatment and claimed the money for her swim, this doctor's nurse shook her head and said to him privately: "I just do not understand how you did it, because we both know that her condition *was* incurable."

Quipped the doctor: "To be the picture of health, one must get into a good frame of mind." How true!

THE IMAGINATION'S FANTASTIC POWER

The imaging faculty of the mind is one of man's most important for his health, wealth and happiness.

Yet it has often been misunderstood and belittled. Because of ignorance of its fantastic power, most of us have been victims of our imagination.

A noted doctor at Harvard Medical School once pointed this out to his medical students. Lecturing on the fantastic power of the imagination, he warned them against imagining that they personally had the diseases they were studying. He stated that medical history is full of examples of people who have made themselves sick through destructive use of the imagination.

This noted medical specialist then cited how misuse of his imagination had made him sick early in his medical career with what he thought was Bright's disease. At that time, he had vividly described every phase of this disease in great detail, while lecturing on the subject. The more he thought about and talked about this disease, the more convinced he became that he was developing it.

The conviction grew so strong that he did not even dare to undergo a physical examination. Instead he lost his appetite, color, energy, weight, and finally was unable to work. Hearing of his condition, a medical friend visited him and was so alarmed at this man's appearance that he offered to examine him. But this doctor replied it would do no good, because he already knew that he had this dreaded disease.

Only after a great deal of persuasion did he finally submit to an examination, which revealed there was not the slightest evidence of disease of any kind. The "patient" then rallied quickly as his appetite, color, energy and weight returned.

Few of us realize the almost superhuman power that

the imagination has upon the body. I know of a fine young doctor who became so engrossed in the study of arthritis, that at an early age he was severely afflicted with that disease.

Medical history shows that people have actually died, because they wrongly used the imagination. These conscientious folks were convinced they had diseases which, in reality, they never had. Their trouble lay not in the body but in the mind.

As the sixteenth century physician, Paracelsus, pointed out: "Imagination is the cause of man's diseases."

Just as the imagination has a fantastic destructive power, so has it a fantastic constructive power, too.

A physician on a fishing trip was summoned to attend another fisherman, who was in pain. The doctor had no medicine case or drugs with him. But knowing of the healing power of the imagination, he made some powders out of ordinary flour and gave careful instructions as to the exact time and manner in which they were to be taken. The patient was also assured by the other fishermen in his party that he was being treated by a noted physician and would feel better shortly.

The remedy wrought such a marvelous change in his condition that in a short time, this man said he could feel the effects of the "medicine" working throughout his body!

While at the theater, a young lady complained of feeling ill. Her escort was a doctor. Upon hearing her complaint, he took something from his pocket and whispered, "Keep this tablet in your mouth, but do not swallow it." Following these directions, she immediately felt better. Later she was curious to know what kind of tablet had relieved her discomfort, yet had not dissolved.

Examination revealed it to be a small button.

HOW THE IMAGINATION HEALS

Why is the picturing faculty of the mind so powerful that it can tear down or build up your health?

Because the imagination is that faculty of the mind which pictures and forms. The imagination is the author of size, weight, form, color. Everything that is visible was first an invisible mental picture, and was brought forth as a tangible result by the picturing power of the mind.

It is well known that the artist sees in his mind every picture he puts on canvas. In like manner, man accumulates a mass of ideas and with his imagination molds them into definite results. It is through the imagination that the formless takes form.

How?

When your imagination flashes its mental pictures into the cells that make up the organs of your body, the brain centers in those cells respond. Out of the substance found within them, they make forms that correspond to the pictures flashed them by the imagination.

For instance, if you are imaging wholeness, your mental picture fixes the idea of wholeness in that invisible mind substance, located right within the cells of your body. The forces of the mind found in the cells then get busy producing that picture of wholeness. If you are picturing some evil condition in your body, through the same process the imagination will build it up in the cells of your body, until it appears as a physical ailment.

AN INCREDIBLE HEALING FORMULA

To picture health is one of the most scientific ways of producing it in the body. To picture health is also one of the quickest roads to healing.

How often I have heard people wail, "I have prayed and prayed for healing. Still my health has not improved." Investigation usually reveals that while these people sorely wanted health, they had not opened their minds to receive it, because they had not pictured it! Thus their prayers had seemed in vain.

According to Latin roots, to "image" means to "conceive," "to become pregnant with," or "to take into one's mind." Just as one cannot give birth to a child until after physical conception has occurred, neither can one give birth to new health until mental conception has occurred. One must first image or conceive it. The image makes the condition. Without the image there can be no condition.

The French doctor, Emile Coué, proved the healing power of the imagination at the turn of the twentieth century. After more conventional methods of treatment had failed, people from all over Europe sought out Dr. Coué for healing. The success of his cures became so widespread that at the height of his career, he treated as many as one hundred people a day.

His method? He deliberately set up the picture of healing in each patient's mind by first assuring him, "Nobody ought to be sick!" Dr. Coué then persisted in making that mental picture firm in the patient's mind by having him affirm daily, "EVERY DAY IN EVERY WAY, I AM GETTING BETTER AND BETTER."

This Frenchman taught that the subconscious mind which controls the body, was most quickly impressed by mental pictures. By changing those mental pictures, one could quickly change the subconscious, and consequently the body which houses it. He proved that the imagination is a much stronger force than the will; that when the imagination and will are in conflict, the imagination can always triumph.

Thus, if your imagination is picturing health, it is possible for that health to manifest in your body, regardless of diagnosis to the contrary or a previous history of ill health. Knowing this, you should deliberately picture yourself as whole and well. The reasoning power of your will may insist that you cannot be healed, but pay it no attention. If you will dare to picture health consistently anyway, then your imagination is free to work for you to produce that health. *Whatever the mind pictures and expects, that it will also build and produce for you!*

WOMAN PAST SEVENTY HEALS HERSELF

There is incredible healing power in this simple formula. *Through deliberate, constructive use of your imagination, you can produce wonderful changes in the body.*

A woman had long suffered nagging health problems which the finest of medical treatment had been unable to clear up. Finally she began to study Truth literature and realized that her health could be restored only after she entertained the picture of health.

In order to "conceive" health mentally, she did a

number of things:

She immediately stopped talking about her aches and pains. She began to read various books on healing. She began taking physical exercises; tried a new diet; and resumed taking the vitamins previously prescribed by her physician. She began to lead a more balanced life of work, play, and rest. She began to work daily in her flower garden, to take sun baths, and to enjoy the fresh air. In all these ways, she was mentally and deliberately conceiving the picture of health.

Next, she made a wheel of fortune, which pictured an active, healthy life. As she viewed her health wheel of fortune daily, she decreed: "I AM THE RADIANT CHILD OF GOD. MY MIND, BODY AND AFFAIRS NOW MANIFEST HIS RADIANT PERFECTION."

She began to praise her body. She also made it a point to praise other people, rather than dwelling upon their faults. She began associating with friends and relatives who were healthy, and who spoke in terms of health. She deliberately terminated her membership in one organization, whose members spent most of their meeting periods discussing their aches and pains.

She made it a point to plan ahead for special events she liked and which she could look forward to: plays, movies, concerts, art exhibits, dinner parties, church events. This helped her to picture herself as healthy enough to attend those planned events.

She constantly blessed her body with health and her life with "divine activity." She daily gave thanks that she was whole and well through and through.

As she worked to deliberately set up the mental picture of health, life, and activity to replace the former beliefs in fatigue, ill health, old age, and inactivity— her mental pictures began to take control of her thoughts, emotions, body and life. She became "pregnant" with the image of health.

In only a matter of weeks, her life began to reflect the beautiful pictures of health and happiness pictured on her wheel of fortune. Later she went on to a new career. Though this lady was more than seventy years "young" when she began picturing a healthy way of life, she proved that through deliberate, constructive use of your imagination, you can produce wonderful changes in your body, and in your life.

NOTHING NEW ABOUT THIS TECHNIQUE

There is nothing new about this theory. Mankind has long known that in order to receive, you must first conceive or picture your desires.

Pre-historic man carved pictures of the food he desired on the walls of his cave. He believed that as he looked often at those pictures, an Unseen Power would attract the food near him in the form of game, fish, fowl. It happened repeatedly.

Twenty-five hundred years ago during the Golden Age of Greece, the cultured Grecians took advantage of this mental law and surounded their prospective mothers with beautiful pictures and statuary, in order that the unborn children might receive pictures of health and beauty from each mother's mind.

HOW A PRINCE'S CROOKED BACK
BECAME STRAIGHT

An old fable has taught the imaging law of healing for many centuries:

Once upon a time there was a prince with a crooked back, who could not stand up straight. One day he summoned the most skillful sculptor in his kingdom, requesting that he make a statue of the prince, true to his likeness in every detail—with one exception. This statue would have a straight back. Explained the prince to the sculptor: "I wish to see myself as I might have been."

When the statue was completed, the prince ordered that it be placed in a secret nook in his palace garden where only he could view it. Daily he stole away from his duties to look longingly upon this statue, paying great attention to the straight back, the uplifted head, and the noble brow.

The days passed into weeks, the weeks into months, and the months into years. Then a strange rumor spread throughout the land: "The prince's back is no longer crooked. Our prince now has the look of a mighty man." When these rumors reached the prince, with a strange smile he went out into the garden where the statue stood. And behold, it was true! His back was as straight as the statue's. His head displayed the same noble bearing. He had become the healthy man his statue had long before pictured him to be.

The Bible contains stories showing how the imaging power of the mind can be used to heal. Among the most familiar is that of Jesus healing the man blind from birth; (John 9) and that of Peter healing the beggar, who had been lame from birth. (Acts 3) How the imagination helped to heal them is explained in my book *The Dynamic Laws of Prosperity*.[1]

---

1. Published by DeVorss & Company, Marina del Rey, CA, rev. ed. 1985.

INTENSITY IS THE SECRET

Imagination is the power to gather thoughts together in new, different arrangements; and to hold so firmly to those new mental pictures that they actually manifest in the body. A friend of mine, the late Reverend Carol Marie Guental, often taught her congregation: "If you can hold it (an idea, mental picture) in your mind, you can hold it in your hand."

Casually picturing good health is not enough. You must persist in holding to that picture. As the prince in the foregoing fable proved, it is when your mental picture reaches a certain level of intensity that your imaging faculty then stamps it with shape and form as improved bodily conditions. Thus, it is the persistent soul that is the most successful in proving the imaging law of healing.

A famed mathematician once said that ideas are vague, nebulous, formless and often remain so, not fulfilling their destiny, unless given definite shape, color, and form by the imaging faculty—which has been described as "the scissors of the mind."

When definite ideas are deliberately pictured by the imaging faculty, they are then able to take shape and expand into precise results in the mind, body and affairs of man. You are constantly experiencing results that correspond to the intensity of your imagination.

Many people give up too easily. If they invoke the imaging law of healing at all, they often do so casually and haphazardly. It is not enough to picture healing. You must concentrate upon that picture to the exclusion of all else. To concentrate means to become "one-pointed" or to rest your mind on an idea. There is no strain connected with it. You simply call your mind back again and again to the picture of health you desire. In this way, you constantly feed the mental picture of health to the brain centers in the cells of your body. Since they have a clear, definite picture to work with, they are able to produce marvelous results for you; whereas lukewarm, half-hearted mental pictures have no intensity and their power for manifestation is limited.

INFECTION, SMOKING, WEIGHT PROBLEMS RESOLVED

In *The Dynamic Laws of Prosperity* is the story of a housewife who proved that intensity is the secret of success in invoking the imaging law of healing.

This housewife had suffered a severe knee infection which, after many weeks, continued to be swollen, infected, and very painful. Unable to gain assurance from others as to its permanent healing, this woman decided to invoke the imaging law of healing.

Every day she began sitting quietly for a time and directing her attention not to the swollen knee, but to the one that was healthy. She would place her hand on the healthy knee, give thanks for its wholeness, and get a strong mental picture of that perfect knee. Daily she continued this mental exercise. When anyone asked about her ailing knee, she conveyed the image of healing to them by always replying that her knee was healing nicely, though at this point her statement was strictly one of faith.

At first there seemed no change in the infected knee, but she persisted in seeing it well. One morning after weeks of pain and swelling, she awakened to find that overnight the swelling had disappeared, the knee had lost all appearance of abnormality, and was again its proper size. Upon closer inspection, it looked as though the skin in that area had been pricked in many places and the infected substance had simply escaped. Her husband, a successful businessman, substantiated her experience to me. They both spoke of how delighted her physician was when he examined her knee and realized that an unusual healing had taken place.

The imaging law of healing can be used to meet all types of problems successfully:

Three businessmen used this method to stop smoking; a woman overcame paralysis; a businessman lost forty excess pounds; and a housewife helped her husband get a healing from alcoholism. There are also countless stories relating financial success acquired through this technique.

In *The Prosperity Secrets of the Ages* are stories relating how marriages, the adoption of children, the sale of property, foreign travel, and domestic help were obtained through imaging.

BEWARE OF DESTRUCTIVE IMAGES

You should watch your deep, inner, secret thoughts. Through them you are setting up intense images that will mold your life in destructive or constructive ways.

There once was a frustrated housewife who did not get along with her husband. Having learned of the imaging power of the mind, she secretly decided that the best way out of her predicament was to picture her husband as dead. In the deep recesses of her mind, she went to work with great intensity on this mental picture.

As she began using her mind in this destructive way,

what she pictured for her husband began to happen to her! It was only after she got critically ill that she realized what she had done. Thereafter, she silently asked her husband's forgiveness and began to entertain healthy thoughts again. She regained her health and learned a valuable lesson:

You can draw to yourself anything you picture. But if you misuse your imaging powers and picture destruction for another, you are personally inviting that destruction into your own life. What you image for another can happen to you, so be careful.

Man's image-making ability came under the early admonitions of the lawgivers of Israel. Many punishments were devised for the "workers of iniquity" who deliberately set up false images.

ERASURE OF DISEASE IMAGES
BRINGS HEALING

Perhaps you wonder how, at times, you have developed diseases you had not consciously pictured for yourself.

When you connect your thinking with a disease atmosphere of any kind, you become susceptible to the effects of that atmosphere, the consciousness of which may contain a number of diseases that you are not aware of.

This is why it is not wise to listen to other people's descriptions of disease, or in other ways to fill your mind with disease ideas, even in an impersonal way. Your imagination takes you seriously and gets busy producing those diseases within you.

Anger, jealousy, possessiveness, resentment, condemnation, hate, and negative thinking of any kind—form disease germs. Continued negative thinking forms large currents of disease germs that are then released within your organism in a mighty stream, thoroughly poisoning it.

For instance, fear generates disease, because fear causes an impression on the subconscious phase of mind which controls so many functions of your body. Unless that fear is removed, you become susceptible to the very diseases you are fearing.

Fortunately, just as imaging can be used to produce disease in the body, it can also be used to erase disease from the body. When you cease to feed or nourish your fears by refusing to think, speak, or listen to anything that pertains to them, you free your mind of such conditions, and thus erase their thought forms in your imagination. *When the image disappears from the mind, its physical equivalent disappears from the body. Permanent healing often begins with the erasure of disease pictures in the mind.*

This has been proved in the case of warts. It has always been a mystery to most people how warts often vanish in a few days when "wished away." When you wish away warts, you are consciously and subconsciously letting go of the picture that had been holding them. You then begin to see yourself free from this condition. The image of warts disappears from your mind and with it, the effect that it had outpictured in your body.

HOW HE MAY HAVE EXTENDED
HIS LIFE 40 YEARS

Charles Fillmore proved that when you cease to feed and nourish negative pictures in the mind, you free yourself of their effect on the body. When Mr. Fillmore was nearing the age of fifty, he wrote:

> About three years ago, the belief in old age began to take hold of me. I was nearing the half-century mark. I began to get wrinkled and gray, my knees tottered, and a great weakness came over me. I did not discern the cause at once, but I found in my dreams I was associating with old people, and it gradually dawned upon me that I was coming into this phase of race belief.
>
> I spent hours and hours silently affirming my unity with the infinite energy of the one true God. I associated with the young, danced with the boys, sang "folk" songs with them, and for a time took on the frivolity of the thoughtless kid. In this way I switched the old-age current of thought.
>
> Then I went deep down within my body and talked to the inner life centers. I told them with firmness and decision that I would never submit to the old age devil, that I was determined never to give in. Gradually I felt a new life current coming up from the life center. It was a faint little stream at first, and months went by before I got it to the surface. Now it is growing strong by leaps and bounds. My cheeks have filled out, the wrinkles and crow's feet are gone, and I actually feel like the boy that I am.[2]

Later, in 1919, at the age of sixty-five, Mr. Fillmore went through an illness so serious that those close to him did not see how he could survive. For months he was unable to work. Yet as he continued affirming and holding to the picture of health, he came out of that near fatal illness with renewed vigor, and lived almost

---

2. James Dillet Freeman, *The Story of Unity.*

thirty years longer. Those last three decades were among the busiest of his entire life.

ACCELERATE YOUR HEALING!

You can hasten, even greatly accelerate, healing through imaging. For this purpose I suggest you make a health wheel of fortune and view it daily, following the instructions given in *The Dynamic Laws of Prosperity*.[3] Like the seventy-year old lady previously mentioned in this chapter, do everything possible to build and live your image of health now. *You should constantly picture better than the best you are now experiencing!*

I recently met a woman who told me that several members of her family had experienced miraculous healings after she secretly made and used a health wheel of fortune for them. Thus your imaging power can prove a blessing to others, too. Why not prove that continuous use of the imagination is powerful enough to create any good thing?

---

3. See also the author's books *Open Your Mind to Prosperity*, chapter 4; and *The Healing Secrets of the Ages*, chapter 7.

THE MYSTICAL LAW
OF HEALING

— Chapter 11 —

An unhealthy woman lamented, "All my problems revolve around other people. If I didn't have to live in a world with people, I would have no problems!"[1]

An unhealthy person is an unhappy person—one who usually has human relations problems. Health problems indicate "people problems."

However, if you have health problems which you know have resulted from the worry connected with troublesome people in your midst, then the mystical law of healing can be your salvation.

It is one of the basic teachings of psychology that all environments, circumstances, conditions and people who come near you, existed first as ideas in your own

---

1. See chapter 5, "Your Gift of a 'People Consciousness,' " in the author's book, *Open Your Mind to Receive.*

mind. One of the great secrets of establishing healthy relationships with others is to learn how to clear inharmonious ideas about them from your own thinking.

The great minds of all ages have known that if you deal exactly right with your own thinking, the people around you will respond with right attitudes and right conditions—either by becoming harmonious in your midst, or by moving out of your life, finding their good elsewhere.

I want to share with you a special method that will help you to deal exactly right in your own thinking with other people. This mystical technique may add years to your life, as it relieves you of unnecessary worry and friction. It can work wonders in your relationships with others. It may even turn enemies into friends. And it will surely add immeasurably to your own mental and physical health.

HOW THIS METHOD WORKS

You can employ this mystical law of healing secretly —with words. True words are angels. True words are alive with power. True words are health-producing, harmony-producing. There is a definite way you can employ words and produce harmonious results:

The ancients felt that every person has an angel or higher self. They felt that when you cannot reach that person's higher self through reasoning with him, or even through the usual methods of prayer, you can reach his higher self by writing to his angel. They believed that the angel of God's Presence is a miracle-working Presence that is available to everyone.

By writing to a person's angel, you establish in your own thinking a harmonious feeling about that person.

Instead of continuing to see him as a person "with horns," that person also has a higher, spiritual self that can be reached, and which will respond harmoniously. Jesus described this higher self in man as "the kingdom of God within you." (Luke 17:21) Paul described it as "Christ in you, the hope of glory." (Colossians 1:27) Abraham Lincoln spoke of it as "the better angels of our nature."

When you begin to think of a troublesome person from this higher standpoint, you radiate thoughts of harmony and good will to that one subconsciously; and you also recognize and thereby bring alive in that person's consciousness his own higher nature, which Job described as "a spirit in man." (Job 32:8)

There is something about written words that reach past the emotional blocks of vanity, ego, pride, deception, intellectual argumentativeness, hurt feelings, inferiority, and that reach deep within to the judgment seat of such people, penetrating their spiritual nature.

YOUNG DOCTOR PROVES THIS METHOD

Although all religions and cultures have long taught that your words have power, many cultures have realized that there is special power in written words. John, in his Revelation, speaks of writing to the angels of the seven churches. (Revelation 2 and 3) Here, the word "church" symbolizes a person's higher self or spiritual consciousness. The seven churches, to whom John wrote, are symbolic of the seven types of people whom you can reach by writing to their angels, when you seem unable to reach them in other ways.

I have known a number of people who used this mystical method of healing for reaching troublesome people and clearing up inharmony, sometimes of long standing. Of course, their own health, wealth and happiness was enhanced as a result.

A young doctor learned of this mystical technique and used it to great advantage. For some months he had been out of harmony with another doctor and had used every means he knew to restore harmony, but the other physician had refused his bids for reconciliation. This man began daily writing to the angel of his former friend, asking that perfect understanding be re-established between them. Several weeks later, he met this doctor friend on the street and, to his surprise, was greeted graciously and invited to lunch! Their friendship was re-established and has continued unhindered since that time.

The word "write" means to "engrave," "to form," "to make a deep and permanent impression." Written words do just that: They make a deep permanent impression upon the ethers of the universe, thereby forming definite results from the ethers.

Written words are an excellent method of healing, because written words also make a deep impression upon the consciousness of those to whom they are written. Many a case of sickness and inharmony would be quietly resolved if someone would write out good words about the people and situations involved.

After only briefly mentioning this angel-writing technique in *The Dynamic Laws of Prosperity*, I was amazed at the amount of mail I received from many readers, who had tested this technique and had proved its power for achieving harmony with others. They were so impressed with the results of their efforts that they requested more detailed instructions that would enable them to employ this mystical law of healing with even greater wisdom.

The seven types of people you can most easily reach by writing to their angels are these:

FIRST: HOW TO REACH THE EXCITABLE TYPE
Unto the angel of the church in Ephesus write.
(Revelation 2:1)

The word "Ephesus" means "desirable," "appealing." You know appealing people who are hard to reach. Their outward life is full of excitement. They are emotional, lovers of amusement, theatrical in their tastes, and dramatic in everything they do. Paul spent three years preaching Truth in Ephesus, because he realized this type was hard to reach and help.

This type makes a fine appearance. They often live beyond their means and have financial as well as health problems. Their health problems usually occur in the ganglionic center at the pit of the stomach, which controls and directs all the organs pertaining to digestion and assimilation.

Philosophers like Darwin and Spencer have said that desire is the root of all body building. They claimed that desire draws together the protoplasmic cells that make the stomach of the most primitive life forms. Desire is another name for constructive thought. When that desire is constructive, it forms healthy cells in the stomach and abdominal region. When that desire is destructive and filled with negative emotion, it causes all kinds of health problems in that region. Thus, when you write to the angel of an Ephesian who has health problems, be sure to bless him with "divine desire."

Write out affirmations such as these:

"I BLESS YOU WITH DIVINE DESIRE AND WITH DIVINE FUL-
FILLMENT. YOU ARE SATISFIED WITH DIVINE LOVE NOW.
HEALTH AND HARMONY ARE NOW ESTABLISHED IN YOUR
MIND, BODY AND AFFAIRS."

The wonderful thing to remember about the people you are trying to help in this category is that they have an intense desire for greater good in their lives, and they will unconsciously respond to the thought of "divine desire and divine fulfillment," since that is what they truly want.

Though they seem unsettled, they are easy to know, having a pleasant, agreeable personality, and they are interested in the finer things of life. By writing to their higher self, stating the Truth about them, you easily reach that deeper phase of their nature, and they happily respond.

In fact, there is no emotional block with this type. They are almost too receptive That is one of their problems. They are receptive to too many things, situations, people, thereby scattering their spiritual forces, and accomplishing nothing.

HOW THE AUTHOR COLLECTED A DEBT

While still in the business world many years ago, I once knew a person of this type. His outer life was exhilarating. He was emotional, and had a flair for the dramatic. He owed me for some work I had done for his firm. Several months had passed and I had not been paid. My affirmations about the immediate, complete payment of this account had not brought satisfactory results.

Finally I remembered the angel-writing technique. One night quite late, I sat and wrote out fifteen times: "TO THE ANGEL OF JOHN BROWN, (let us say) I BLESS YOU AND GIVE THANKS THAT YOU ARE HANDLING THIS FINANCIAL MATTER PROMPTLY, AND THAT I AM IMMEDIATELY AND COMPLETELY PAID." The reason I wrote out this statement fifteen times was because the mystics of old believed that fifteen was the number that would dissolve adversity and break up hard conditions.

After writing out this statement, I felt much better about the situation and was able to completely release it from my mind. Two days later, my friend telephoned to say his bookkeeper was writing my check, and that I would receive it by mail the following day, which I did.

SECOND: HOW TO REACH THE BITTERSWEET TYPE
And to the angel of the church in Smyrna write.
(Revelation 2:8)

The word "Smyrna" means "flowing substance," "sweet," "fragrant," "aromatic." It also means "bitterness," "gall," "sorrow," "lamentation," "rebellion." And these words well describe this type.

Like the Ephesians, Symrnians make a fine appearance. They are also lovers of show, beauty, adornment. They live beyond their means and usually have financial problems. When things go their way, they are sweet, harmonious people. But when they do not get their way, their personalities reverse and they become rebellious, bitter and lament their lot in life.

The word "Smyrna" metaphysically means "substance" and since the substance center in the body is located in the stomach, these people usually have stomach trouble. As they misuse the substance of their thoughts and emotions in bitterness, rebellion, and willfulness, their acid feelings react upon the chemicals of the body; this type also misuses their financial substance in high living. This, too, can react upon the substance center in the stomach.

This type needs to let go of personal willfulness so that the divine plan for their lives can unfold. It is good to affirm for them: "NOT YOUR WILL BUT GOD'S WILL IS BEING DONE IN, THROUGH AND ROUND ABOUT YOU NOW. YOU WILLINGLY DO THE WILL OF GOD, WHICH IS FOR YOUR SUPREME GOOD."

To help uplift the substance of their thoughts and feelings, and its consequent reaction upon their health, write out affirmations such as these:

"YOU ARE SATISFIED WITH DIVINE SUBSTANCE. DIVINE SUBSTANCE IS DOING ITS PERFECT WORK IN YOUR MIND, BODY, AFFAIRS AND RELATIONSHIPS NOW. DIVINE SUBSTANCE HEALS YOU NOW."

HOW A DIVORCED MAN GOT HIS WIFE BACK

A businessman was having great difficulty with his wife, who had divorced him. He was heartbroken because he still loved her. He had tried to talk with her about reconciliation, but she was very confused, and he could not reason with her.

He learned of the mystical method of healing and was fascinated with the technique, realizing that his wife was this second type. Her appearance was stylish and she loved beautiful, showy fashions. In fact, this very issue had been one of their basic problems. Her tastes had been much too expensive for his pocketbook.

He began nightly writing to her angel, asking help in straightening out their marriage. One day, after not having heard from her for some time, she contacted him, tearfully declaring that their divorce had been a mistake. They quietly remarried, and this man effortlessly maintained peace and harmony with his wife by continuing to secretly write to her angel.

THIRD: HOW TO REACH THE ALOOF INTELLECTUAL TYPE
And to the angel of the church in Pergamum write.
(Revelation 2:12)

The word "Pergamum" means "strongly united," "closely knit." This is the grand, aristocratic type—literary, scientific, artistic, lovers of society and statescraft, often disdainful of spiritual subjects, having faith only in "reason."

This type is strongly united, closely knit in family, social, intellectual, and business relationships. The Pergamums are suspicious of new people, new ideas, new ways of doing things. They do not want anything or anybody to interfere with their reasonable, well-ordered lives and theories.

The Pergamum symbolizes metaphysically the intellectual consciousness of man, which is filled with human intelligence, but which is often closed to the higher wisdom of divine understanding and intuition.

Since the center of divine understanding in man is located in the forehead just above the eyes, this type often has headaches and eye trouble. As they view life from a human, limited, reasonable standpoint, their limited vision is reflected in their eyesight and other health problems of that area.

When you write to this type, be sure to bless them with divine intelligence:

"YOU ARE LETTING DIVINE INTELLIGENCE EXPRESS PER-
FECTLY THROUGH YOU NOW. YOU SEE WITH THE EYES OF
SPIRIT. YOU HAVE UNLIMITED VISION FOR SEEING AND EX-
PERIENCING THE GOOD. YOU ARE OPEN AND RECEPTIVE TO
YOUR HIGHEST GOOD NOW IN THE FORM OF NEW IDEAS,
NEW UNDERSTANDING, NEW EXPERIENCES."

HOW HE SUCCESSFULLY MARRIED INTO
A CLOSE-KNIT FAMILY

A young man fell in love and wanted to marry. But the girl of his choice was from a close-knit family that did not want to release her emotionally. This family group was suspicious of new people and new ways of doing things. In fact, they strongly united against the invasion of anything new in their lives. The young man realized that from a human standpoint, it appeared hopeless to try to win this girl, even though she was in love with him, too.

It was at this point that he learned of the mystical law of healing. He immediately wrote to her angel, and to the angel of her family, decreeing for her emotional freedom, a happy marriage between them, and asking that her family would divinely adjust to this change graciously.

For some months he continued nightly this angel-writing technique with no visible results. Then suddenly everything changed. He could sense a freedom that had not previously existed. He proposed and they quickly married. Though it took her family some time to make their adjustment and to emotionally accept him into the family, they finally did so wholeheartedly. Until they did, he continued to write to their angel.

FOURTH: HOW TO REACH THE ZEALOUS-QUARRELSOME TYPE
And to the angel of the church in Thyatira write.
(Revelation 2:18)

"Thyatira" means "rushing headlong," "frantic." This type is zealous, quarrelsome, easily offended. They have greater ideals than inner ability for producing idealistic results. Their resulting frustration flares up in temperamental behavior.

Metaphysically, the word "Thyatira" symbolizes the intense desire of the soul for the higher expressions of life. The zeal center in the body is located at the back of the neck. The health problems of Thyatirans center in the back of the head and spine. When you write to this type, decree for them "peace, poise, power." Affirm that their zeal is tempered with wisdom.

The sicknesses, pains, and thousand-and-one inharmonies and discords that come to this type of person result because of his zealous desire to do things on his own quickly, frantically, apart from wisdom. In the process he scatters his forces and dissipates the substance of his thoughts and emotions. This dissipation manifests as physical and emotional discord.

In writing to this type affirm for him: "YOU ARE NOW
BLESSED WITH PEACE, POISE, POWER. YOUR ZEAL IS TEM-
PERED WITH WISDOM. YOU REST AND RELAX IN DIVINE WIS-
DOM, AND YOU ARE SHOWN THE WAY. YOU ARE STRONG IN
THE LORD AND IN THE POWER OF HIS MIGHT."

HOW HARSH TREATMENT WAS OVERCOME

Thyatirans are often interested in athletics. A housewife learned that the instructor at a health club was
being harsh with the teenage boys whom he was in-
structing. Though her son and his friends were upset
by this harsh treatment, they did not wish her to interfere, feeling that would bring only more scorn from
their unhappy instructor. This mother asked these
teenagers to begin nightly writing to the angel of the
instructor, decreeing fair treatment and more understanding. She joined them in this angel-writing project.

For a time no results appeared. Then suddenly the
instructor announced he was leaving this job to take a
better one at a nearby college. Along with an increased
income, the new job would allow him time to work on
his master's degree, which had long been his desire.

This mother then realized that this health instructor's harsh treatment had apparently stemmed from
his own frustration and job dissatisfaction. Thus he
had become quarrelsome, easily offended and cruel to
those about him.

The final result of this angel-writing project was
that this lady's son won a trophy from this health club
—which was topped by the figure of an angel!

FIFTH: HOW TO REACH THE FEARFUL BODY
DEVOTEES

And to the angel of the church in Sardis write.
(Revelation 3:1)

The word "Sardis" means "prince of joy." This is the timid, apprehensive type. These are the body devotees. They are afraid of draughts, accidents, and even of what they eat. They are always seeking the comfortable, soft, pleasant things of bodily life. No books, lessons or instructions seem to quench their fear, but writing to their angels brings out the bold, brave, dauntless spirit within them, so that they become, as the word "Sardis" implies, "princes of joy" and power.

This type is always changing his mind. In his health, the power center located in the throat is his weak spot. He develops sore throats, colds, loss of voice, and other congestion in that area, whenever he becomes fearful or upset.

This kind of person has great potential for becoming a powerful individual in his chosen field. You awaken that power center within him, bringing it alive, through writing to his angel. This gives him a stability and fearlessness which he needs in order to express his potential power.

To the Sardis type, write: "ALL POWER IS GIVEN UNTO YOU IN MIND, BODY, AFFAIRS AND RELATIONSHIPS. THE POWER OF GOD IS WORKING THROUGH YOU TO FREE YOU FROM EVERY NEGATIVE INFLUENCE. NOTHING CAN HOLD YOU IN BONDAGE. ALL POWER IS YOURS TO CONTROL YOUR THOUGHTS, TO VITALIZE YOUR BODY, TO GAIN SUCCESS, TO BLESS OTHERS. YOU NOW UNLEASH YOUR DIVINE POWERS. YOU KNOW WHAT TO DO AND YOU DO IT!"

HOW HE BROUGHT A LONG-STANDING
BUSINESS MATTER TO COMPLETION

A businessman was having difficulty trying to bring a business matter to a conclusion. It had been pending a long time. Everyone involved was congenial and wished the matter completed, except one man who kept changing his mind. He was unsure about every aspect of the situation.

The businessman wishing to conclude things heard of the angel-writing method and realized that the person who kept changing his mind was this type—timid, apprehensive, fearful, unsure. He wrote to this man's angel, asking that the business matter be brought to an early, appropriate conclusion in which all involved would be satisfied and blessed.

A few days later the man who had stalled for so long visited this businessman and said, "Come down to my office tomorrow morning and the papers will be ready to sign." Then he added, as though it was his own idea, "This situation has been delayed long enough and I am anxious to conclude it."

SIXTH: HOW TO REACH THE LOVING-WORKS TYPE
And to the angel of the church in Philadelphia write.
(Revelation 3:7)

The word "Philadelphia" means "brotherly love," "fraternal love," "universal love." This type talks much about the brotherhood of man, but love to them means outer works alone, rather than an inner consciousness of love and peace.

These are the philanthropists of human existence. Community organizations, clubs, fraternal groups, civic groups, churches are all filled with people seeking to give and receive brotherly love. Philadelphians are inclined to express love from the personal level alone, often exhausting themselves in loving works. They work to be "seen of men," which Jesus warned against. Their type of love is usually dominated by selfishness, rather than by selflessness. When they feel their efforts are unappreciated, they become unloving in their thoughts and actions. Strife, hatred, and warring emotions then take over, and the love center in the body, located in the heart, is affected. This is why heart trouble often occurs in the busy, "loving works" type.

In writing to the Philadelphians, decree that they become loving in their thoughts, since that is the place where all true love begins: "YOU ARE THE PERFECT EXPRESSION OF DIVINE LOVE. DIVINE LOVE TRANSFORMS YOU. DIVINE LOVE FILLS YOUR HEART WITH HARMONY AND YOUR MIND WITH PEACE. YOU ARE LOVED AND APPRECIATED BY GOD AND MAN."

If you find yourself in a group or organization where the loving works do not seem balanced by an inner consciousness of love, you can write to the angel of that organization, asking that divine love come alive in the thoughts, as well as in the actions, of that group. As you do this, those people who are not in tune with divine love will fade harmoniously out of the group, and those who are lovingly in tune with its aims and purposes will appear. In this quiet, secret way, both inner and outer harmony can be established and maintained for the good of all concerned.

HOW HE DISSOLVED ORGANIZATIONAL INHARMONY

An executive found himself in the midst of organizational inharmony. He was not sure just who was responsible for the unrest and critical attitudes found in this group. He tried various methods for re-establishing harmony, but the group remained aloof, critical, inharmonious.

In desperation, he began to daily write to the angel of that organization, asking for help in re-establishing a consciousness of love. Then he wrote: "I CAST THIS BURDEN ON THE ANGEL OF DIVINE LOVE. THE ANGEL OF DIVINE LOVE NOW COMES ALIVE IN THIS SITUATION AND IN ALL PERSONS CONNECTED WITH THIS ORGANIZATION. THE ANGEL OF DIVINE LOVE NOW REIGNS SUPREME."

Soon several volunteer workers resigned their jobs and left the organization, while new workers appeared who were eager to contribute to the progress of the organization in a harmonious way. Thereafter, peace and progress were established and maintained.

SEVENTH: HOW TO REACH THE UNSTABLE WANDERERS
And to the angel of the church in Laodicea write.
(Revelation 3:14)

The word "Laodicea" means "justice" and "judgment." This type often has an injustice complex. They are unstable, unsettled, changeable; they are the wanderers seeking new doctrines and new places. They change their religious beliefs and political views often. They are restless, critical, temperamental. They often lament that they have been wronged and misused.

You find this type of person going from one job to another; from one club to another; from one church to another; and sometimes from one marriage to another. They are the "joiners" who do not remain with anything long enough to discover whether it will benefit them or not.

The health problems of the Laodiceans are usually found in the stomach and solar plexus region, because the judgment center in the body is located there. Since dominant memory cells are located in the stomach, and since Laodiceans are constantly remembering unjust experiences, their memorable "wronged" attitudes play havoc in the stomach area. This is why people with an injustice complex usually suffer from stomach trouble.

When you write to this type, decree that the divine law of justice is doing its perfect work in their lives; and that they are being divinely guided into their right place: "YOUR JUSTICE COMES FROM GOD, AND YOU TRUST HIM TO REGULATE ALL YOUR AFFAIRS. DIVINE JUSTICE NOW ADJUSTS EVERY FUNCTION OF YOUR BODY AND EVERY DETAIL OF YOUR LIFE. YOU ARE NOW GUIDED INTO YOUR RIGHT PLACE WHERE YOU ARE DIVINELY SECURE."

The Laodicean will unconsciously respond to your high vision of rightness and stability for him, since he is of a highly sensitive and receptive nature.[2]

THE IMPORTANCE OF PATIENCE
AND SECRECY

In writing to another's angel, at times it will look as though this method is not working. Then suddenly

---

2. See chapter 14, "How to Overcome Injustice" in the author's book, *The Prosperity Secrets of the Ages.*

everything will shift, changes will come, and matters that had seemed destined for failure will clear up very quickly.

You should write to another's angel as often as you feel inclined to until results appear. It is good to address your notes "to the angel of John Brown," then, ask his help concerning that person. It is also good to write out affirmations directly to the person whom you wish to reach. Be very quiet about what you are doing, however, since this is a secret technique that has power only if you keep it a secret. After writing your notes, either burn them or seal them, putting them away in a safe place, while you secretly await results. Be sure to eventually destroy them, so that secrecy shall be preserved.

THE RESULTS OF CALLING ON ONE'S GUARDIAN ANGEL

The word "angel" means "messenger of God." When it seems that your life is filled with defeat, or that you are tempted to condemn yourself, do not overlook writing to your own angel. The office of the angels is to guard, guide and direct you. Allow them that high and holy privilege.

Emma Curtis Hopkins has written in her book, *High Mysticism*:

> The Angel of His Presence accompanies every man.
> . . . This high leadership is every man's heritage. He need not fear dangerous days or vicious circumstances while he is aware that His angel goes before him, pleads his cause and defends him.[3]

---

3. Published by DeVorss & Company, Marina del Rey, CA 90294.

When challenges arise, say to yourself, "I have nothing to fear. My guardian angel goes before me, making right my way." Decree this often for others, too. A businesswoman was concerned about having to make an out-of-town buying trip, since she would have to drive two hundred miles in rain and fog accompanied by her sick husband, whom she could not leave at home alone. A friend said, "You have nothing to fear, because your guardian angel will be with you."

Upon returning from the buying trip, this businesswoman reported, "I did seem to be accompanied by an angel. As I drove out of town, the sky cleared of fog, the rain stopped, and the sun shone through. There was no more bad weather on the entire trip. The drive helped my husband's spirits and he suffered no ill effects from it. Financially, this proved to be the most profitable buying trip I have made in a long time."

Never expect your angel or that of another to honor any requests that might hurt or harm. Be willing that something infinitely better than that which you have in mind comes forth as you use the angel-writing technique. You then open the way for your highest good, as well as for the highest good of all involved, to manifest in an unlimited way.

OTHER SPECIFIC ANGELS WHO CAN HELP YOU

The Hebrews of old felt that Raphael was the angel of healing. At times you may wish to decree: "Angel of Health, come forth here and now!" Or you may wish to

_____

SPECIAL NOTE: For a free copy of the author's "How to Write to the Angel" outline, please write her.

call on the Angel of Prosperity or the Angel of Love
and Harmony in the same way.[4]

A powerful way to invoke the mystical law of healing
is to meditate often upon the promise of the Psalmist,
who companioned the angels:

> There shall no evil befall thee, Neither shall any
> plague come nigh thy tent. For he will give his angels
> charge over thee, To keep thee in all thy ways.
>
> (Psalms 91:10,11)

---

4. For additional information on other specific angels that can
help you, see chapter 5 of the author's book, *The Prospering
Power of Love.*

CHEMICALIZATION, A HEALING PROCESS

— Chapter 12 —

A civil service employee in a distant city once said, "I have your book, *The Dynamic Laws of Prosperity*, and it is the best book on the subject I have ever read. For a time, I worked with the laws you described and they brought dynamic good into my life. But suddenly, I am frightened and discouraged. The last few weeks, everything seems to have gone in reverse. What has happened?"

That lady was relieved to learn that another dynamic law was working for her—the healing law of chemicalization.

You've heard it said that things have to get worse sometimes before they can get better. The getting worse process is actually a part of the improvement process, and what seems failure is actually success being born in the situation. That's chemicalization!

RIGHT THOUGHT PRODUCES CHEMICAL CHANGE

A doctor once told me that he often explained this healing law to his patients. He would point out to them that after beginning treatment, they would probably feel worse before they felt permanently better; that such an experience was nothing to fear; that they could actually rejoice if they did begin to feel worse, because they could then know it was a sign of healing taking place.

Did you ever put soda in an acid fluid and witness the agitation or excited action that took place? *One of the substances neutralized the other, and something better resulted from the action, didn't it?*

This is often what happens in the minds and bodies of people when they begin to deliberately practice the dynamics of right thought. *A chemical change literally takes place in their thoughts and feelings, which is then reflected in their bodies and affairs.*

They may feel nervous, frightened, agitated. If they have ever been sick, their old diseases may flare up again. If they have been morally bad, the old desires and habits may take possession of them again. If they have had previous financial problems, all at once things may seem darker and more hopeless than ever. In their human relationships, it may seem that everybody has turned against them and that inharmony is the order of the day.

What has happened?

Simply this: These people, for years have lived in wrong thought, and molded these negative notions into their bodies and affairs. Now they have begun to do an about-face, thinking in terms of love, praise, forgiveness, release. Such reversed thoughts are a big dose for their system to take, and so there is a clash between their old and new ways of thinking—this sets up a chemical reaction in mind, body and affairs.

At such times the good thing to remember is that one positive thought is more powerful than a thousand, rowdy negative thoughts; the old way of thinking is on its way out, no matter how much noise it makes in the process. It has to go! But having been in control for so long, it doesn't give up without a fight. Even while it is flaring up for the last time, you can know that it is actually unconditionally surrendering and will soon be gone completely. Meanwhile, there seems to be a lot of excitement as it takes its last stand.

HOW TO MEET CHEMICALIZATION VICTORIOUSLY

Chemicalization sounds like a negative process, but is actually a very positive and natural one. Though it is uncomfortable, it is worth going through, because it is a sign that cleansing is taking place. Something higher and better always results from this experience.

When these periods come, remind yourself, "THIS IS NOTHING TO FEAR. THIS IS NOT EVIL. THERE IS ONLY GOOD AT WORK IN THIS EXPERIENCE. HEALING IS NOW TAKING PLACE IN MY WORLD. I REST, RELAX AND LET IT." As you nonresistantly meet chemicalization in this way, very soon brighter conditions will appear.

Emmet Fox has described the healing process of chemicalization:

It seems as though everything begins to go wrong at once. This may be disconcerting, but it is really a good sign. Suppose your whole world seems to rock on its foundation. Hold on steadily, and let it rock, and when the rocking is over, the picture will have reassembled itself into something much nearer to your heart's desire.[1]

Chemicalization means that things are working out better than ever before. Regardless of what seems to be happening, it never means anything else. When a physical or mental disturbance arises after your deliberate use of right thinking, it is always a sign that your right thinking is at work—clearing out the negative, so that the positive power of good can gain complete dominion of your world.

As you practice the prosperity laws given my books, *The Dynamic Laws of Prosperity*, and *The Prosperity Secrets of the Ages*, faithfully writing out your desires, making a wheel of fortune, commanding your good to appear, creating a master plan for success, tithing, and as you practice the healing laws given in this book, faithfully invoking denial, forgiveness, release, and affirmations of love, praise, etc.—don't be surprised if your world begins to rock!

When it does, say to yourself, "This is good! Those laws are working for me in a dynamic way. Only dynamic good shall come from this cleansing experience." You are having a mental, emotional and perhaps even a physical "spring cleaning." How free, unburdened, and ready for better health and greater good you will be as this cleansing perfects you and your world.

---

1. *Around the Year With Emmet Fox*, published by Harper & Bros., N.Y., 1952.

HOW CHEMICALIZATION HEALS

I once gave a series of four lectures on chemicalization, spaced a week apart. Within those four weeks, everybody attending the lectures got a reaction. Things got so stirred up that I wondered if I should continue. But I'm glad I did, because deep-seated situations of long standing came to the surface of the lives of those attending. Those deep-seated conditions flared up, then faded away completely.

More things got straightened out for more people in that short length of time than in any other comparable period of lectures that I can recall. But there was a lot of excitement in the process! The cleansing seemed to work furiously, fast, and then completely.

A lady who was attending that series had long had trouble with her teeth and gums. She was trying to get a spiritual healing. She feared going to a dentist because she knew he would insist on removing all her teeth, and she wanted to save them, if possible.

Off and on her teeth and gums had bothered her, but as she had learned to affirm health they had gotten better. Then she attended the chemicalization lectures. Soon she had to go to bed because the pain, swelling, and fever had again appeared. Her husband wanted to call in their doctor. She refused saying, "This is nothing to fear. I am chemicalizing. I am getting a complete healing in my mouth. I am letting the words of my mouth and the meditations of my heart become acceptable in God's sight." (from the 51st Psalm)

This lady had been very critical of other people and felt that her strong words of criticism had something to do with her bad teeth. She was in and out of bed for several weeks. But she came through the experience victoriously. Her mouth and gums healed completely and she did not lose her teeth.

A businessman once described chemicalization in this way:

"When you have been going in reverse, it is hard to shift into forward gear, without getting a grinding of the gears and a lurching of the vehicle." When that grinding-lurching process starts, after you have shifted forward in your thinking, remind yourself that deep-seated, hard, fixed states of mind filled with strong fears, prejudices, willfulness, jealousy, resentment, unforgiveness, and hate have gotten stirred up as you have begun to think in a higher and better way. Those hard states of mind do not like to be broken up and dissolved—though, of course, they will be as you persist in shifting forward in your thinking, and then remain in that forward mental gear.

THE SURPRISES OF CHEMICALIZATION

Chemicalization is a sign that things are working out for you better than ever before, but chemicalization has other surprises, too. *You may start working mentally to change your thinking about one department of your life, and you may get a chemicalization in another area, without realizing there is a mental correspondence.*

A fine businessman had worked long, hard hours for years in work that was rather negative and very demanding. He had long wanted to leave that field, but having a family to support, he did not know how to make the break. For a time, as he prayed about it and worked mentally for freedom from that job and for his right place in life, nothing happened.

Then one day, his health broke completely. He had to be hospitalized; then followed a long period of convalescence. He knew that somehow this experience was good; that it was trying to lead him into greater good. After his recovery, his doctor assured him that return to his old job would probably kill him.

He was then forced into a new line of work, which is seasonal. He now works about six months of the year; and in that six months, he makes more money than he had previously made working around the clock twelve months of the year.

But things got worse before they got better for that man, and though the chemicalization worked first in his health, it also brought forth a better job, more prosperity and greater freedom in every phase of his life.

Chemicalization results when an old set of ideas, an old way of life, tries to hold on, while a new and better way of thinking and living is trying to appear. This man proved it.

HOW OFTEN ONE EXPERIENCES CHEMICALIZATION

Perhaps you are wondering how often one has to go through this chemicalization process, and if everyone has this experience as they improve their thinking. Usually there is a big chemicalization soon after a person begins to seriously uplift his thinking. If he does not become frightened, but continues through this "initiation," that first big chemicalization is often the greatest he will experience.

There are lesser chemicalizations as one continues to change his thinking, but nothing as severe as that first one. In due time, one has cleared up dominant negative thought patterns in the subconscious mind to the extent that chemicalizations rarely occur. The only exception to this tapering off process is that usually just before or after you make a master demonstration,[2] there is usually a big chemicalization. This is necessary for freeing you of old ways of thinking and living, so that your master demonstration which contains new patterns of good, can come to you.

Does everyone chemicalize? Usually to some degree, as thought patterns change and improve. Just as Jesus had to go through the crucifixion (which symbolizes chemicalization and a crossing out of negation) before He could experience the resurrection, so must we. Strong-willed, aggressive persons of much personality, deep prejudices, and emphatic opinions usually chemicalize much more than persons of milder, more nonresistant, adaptable attitudes toward life.

FIRST STEP IN CHEMICALIZATION: SATURATION

From having observed this cleansing process work in the lives of numerous people, I am convinced that there are four steps in chemicalization. Knowing these steps, you will recognize them as they come, be able to go through them fearlessly, and accept vast improvement in your life thereafter.

---

2. See the chapter "How to Make Your Master Demonstration" in *The Prosperity Secrets of the Ages.*

The first step in chemicalization occurs when you start reading, studying, denying limitation, and affirming greater good for your life. As the saturation of these ideas sets in, then comes the "stirring up" of old ideas, opinions, relationships, health problems, financial affairs, memories of past unhappiness. When this happens, don't be like the woman who began to affirm the good, and as she did, a lot of old things flared up in her life. So she stopped her mental work. Later she began making her affirmations again, and again came the stirring up. This time she gave up completely. As she did, she stopped her good because she refused to go quietly through this cleansing process which would have led her out of a rut of limitation into a life of vast improvement.

When this "stirring up" process begins, do not panic. Just rejoice and give thanks that a deep cleansing is taking place, which is the first step toward greater good. Meet it peacefully and non-resistantly, saying to yourself, "None of these things move me," and "This, too, shall pass," as you continue to study and affirm the good. In this way you become the *victor*, rather than the *victim*, of chemicalization.

SECOND STEP IN CHEMICALIZTION: COMMOTION

The second step in chemicalization is the period in which things really get exciting. The commotion sets in. Already there has been the "stirring-up" period. Now things aren't only stirred up; they shake up and break up. This is usually a loud experience where everyone gets into the act and has their say.

This is your crucifixion (crossing out) of the old, dis-satisfying patterns of thought, methods of living, and relationships which you have outgrown, so that you may get ready for a glorious resurrection of new good that is on the way!

During this shaking-up, breaking-up period, there may be the desertion of family, friends, and even of the usual means of livelihood. In any event, it is a time of confusion, indecision, lack of mental or emotional authority. You just don't feel in control of your world because it is shifting and changing so at this point. Old conditions may reappear and flare up in mind and body. Inharmony may flare up in family relationships. Hard conditions may flare up in financial matters.

A lady doctor once stated that every time she started using prosperity affirmations, her practice went into a decline and her patients did not pay their accounts. A housewife wrote that every time she used prosperity af-firmations, it caused a lot of commotion in her family, though no one knew what she was doing.

Both these people were experiencing the commotion that comes in the second step of chemicalization. They were advised to quietly keep right on affirming pros-perity, knowing that as they did, the excitement would fade away, the patients would pay, and the family would become more harmonious than ever. This is ex-actly what happened.

When the breaking up of limitation begins in your world, causing excitement and commotion, remind yourself that this is but a step in the birth of new good. The attainment of your heart's desires comes after these breaking up, shaking up experiences. So don't back down to appearances. Say to the excitement "PEACE, BE STILL." To your anxious thoughts decree:

"BE STILL AND KNOW THAT GREAT GOOD IS AT WORK IN THIS EXPERIENCE. HEALING IS TAKING PLACE. VAST IMPROVEMENT IS ON THE WAY. IN FACT, VAST IMPROVEMENT COMES QUICKLY IN ALL MY AFFAIRS NOW."

CHEMICALIZATION RESOLVES MARITAL TRIANGLE

A man was involved with a married woman. He had met her while she was separated from her husband, whom she was presumably divorcing. She had seemed his ideal. Their common interests and congeniality had made for a happy courtship.

Then her husband reappeared on the scene, asked her to go back to him, and she promptly did so. It left her suitor heartbroken.

Since her marriage was not happy after she returned to her husband, she got her kicks emotionally by continuing to see this other man. He was so in love with her that he did not have the courage or emotional stamina to break off their relationship, though he realized no good would come of such a triangle.

It was at this point that he sought counseling and was advised to use these affirmations for a perfect solution: "DIVINE LOVE, EXPRESSING THROUGH ME, NOW DRAWS TO ME ALL THAT IS NEEDED TO MAKE ME HAPPY AND MY LIFE COMPLETE. ALL THAT IS NOT FOR MY HIGHEST GOOD NOW FADES OUT OF MY LIFE QUICKLY AND HARMONIOUSLY. DIVINE LOVE CANNOT BE WITHHELD FROM ME. DIVINE LOVE CANNOT BE TAKEN FROM ME. DIVINE LOVE IS THE ONE AND ONLY REALITY IN MY LIFE AND QUICKLY MANIFESTS IN APPROPRIATE FORM HERE AND NOW AS IT PRODUCES PERFECT RESULTS."

As he began to fill his mind with these ideas, chemicalization set in! A friend confidentially informed him that his lady-love was not only seeing him on the side, but that she was enjoying the company of several men too, none of whom her husband knew about. He refused to believe this about his "ideal" until proof was given him.

When it was, this proved to be a breaking-up, shaking-up experience for this man, which caused him to emotionally release this woman. Though it seemed a painful experience, in the turmoil that followed he also released many other unhappy emotional memories of the past.

Thereafter he felt free, unburdened, released from an impossible situation. It was then that great improvement took place: He met and soon happily married the girl of his dreams who was even more congenial, talented and suited to him than the former sweetheart had appeared to be. But this great improvement did not take place until this man went through the breaking-up, shaking-up phase of chemicalization.

THIRD STEP IN CHEMICALIZATION: QUIETNESS

Then comes the third step in chemicalization when things get just as quiet as they have previously been loud. This is a period of apparent loss or failure. This is a readjustment period, a time of great change. And it is a quiet period, which by this time, you welcome!

During this transition period, if there is loss, failure, change, or readjustment quietly facing you, remember this great truth: *When a right-thinking person seems to lose something, it is because his inner self is clearing the way for better things!* This is the time to remind yourself of the ancient truth that when the half-gods go, the gods arrive; and that when the angels go out, the arch-angels come in.

Thus when periods of apparent loss or failure come to you, after you have adopted success attitudes, this is merely a transition period from lesser to greater good. Meet it gracefully, expecting great things to come from this transition period. You will not be disappointed. Do not get frightened or discouraged, thereby postponing your master demonstration. If one particular blessing leaves you, it may be that you had become self satisfied and had ceased to grow. Your soul is now reaching toward greater expansion, and a vacuum had to be formed to make room for that expansion.

At such times, if you do not voluntarily get out of the rut, after you have learned what is necessary for your growth along certain lines, it is as though that cherished blessing drops away from you in order that there may be room for further growth. *Anything, or any experience that causes you to grow, is success and healing taking place!*[3]

You may feel stripped and bare during this third phase of chemicalization, because something new is being born within you, something new is taking place. Your soul is reaching out for greater growth, greater good. Something has dropped away from you, in order to make room for the bigger blessings that are even now on the way!

Meet this quiet transition period of apparent loss or failure by saying to yourself: "I GIVE THANKS FOR DIVINE

---

3. Also see chapter "A Flood Can Be a Healing" in the author's book, *The Prosperity Secrets of the Ages.*

FULFILLMENT, WHICH IS NOW TAKING PLACE. GREATER
GOOD IS ON THE WAY. MY HEART'S DESIRES ARE NOW BE-
ING REALIZED AND FULFILLED."

Let go all ideas of loss or fear of loss. Realize that
whatever has been taken from you will be divinely restored. As you let go what has already gone from your
life, you make way for better things. So rest from trying to do anything or make anything right during this
quiet transition period. Just keep quiet. Do not talk
about the apparent loss or failure that you have just
experienced. If others become aware that changes are
taking place in your life, confidently declare: "ALL IS
WELL." To yourself say often, "I LET GO WHAT GOES.
DIVINE RESTORATION, DIVINE FULFILLMENT IS NOW TAKING
PLACE." As you hold to these healing attitudes, you will
be richly rewarded.

It is imperative that you keep quiet about all that is
happening to you during this period, because your
consciousness is like that of a newborn child that needs
to be quietly protected, so that it may grow strong in
its new understanding. After a while, you begin to feel
in control of your world again. A divine pattern for
your new good begins to unfold to you. Suddenly you
can see why it has all been necessary.

FOURTH STEP IN CHEMICALIZATION: FULFILLMENT

Now comes the final phase of chemicalization. This,
too, is a quiet period at first. This is the period when
the new good begins to appear in your world quietly
and satisfyingly. Nothing spectacular happens. It comes
through a natural unfoldment of ideas and events. As
it does, you recognize it as your dream coming true.

But instead of excitedly wanting to shout your good news to the world, you will probably surprise yourself by being very silent about it. You may find that you actually do not want to talk about it.

And you are wise, because your new found good also needs to be protected, nourished, strengthened, and sheltered from the world. As you quietly nourish it, it waxes strong, grows, expands, and increases.

Once something I had long desired came to me. Its appearance in my life was truly a master demonstration. But I found that when this demonstration actually arrived, instead of being profoundly excited, I could not even talk about it. I was grateful and thankful, but somehow discussion of it just didn't seem appropriate.

In this last phase of chemicalization, as your new good appears, if you talk about it to others, it may dissipate and dissolve; you may lose it completely. So keep quiet and let it grow and expand. As it does, there will be no need for you to "show it off" to the world. Its appearance in your life will be obvious enough.

As this fourth phase of chemicalization appears, it is good to make firm and permanent your new blessings by decreeing often: "DIVINE FULFILLMENT HAS NOW MANIFESTED IN MY LIFE AND AFFAIRS, AND ALL IS WELL. DIVINE FULFILLMENT IS MINE NOW."

This nails down and secures your demonstration. You will realize how worthwhile it was, going through the other three steps of chemicalization, to reach this point of supreme new good. In fact, as you reflect upon all that happened to bring you to this point, you will admit that you would not have missed it for anything; that it has been worthwhile.

Chemicalization, for you, has proved a healing process, as well as a blessing.

YOUR GIVING CAN HEAL YOU!

Chapter 13

Emerson has said, "It is impossible for a man to be cheated by anyone but himself." If you are in ill health, you have unwittingly cheated yourself in some way.

The word "give" in its root means "to have" or "to cause to have." The basic law of life is that you must first give before you can have or receive. This law applies to your health, as well as to your pocketbook. Giving can make you rich. Giving can also heal you!

When you give, you release the dammed up substance within your thoughts, feelings, and body temple. If you are in ill health, there is a block somewhere that is damming up the life force within you. Giving releases that block.

Your flesh, blood, bones, as well as your thoughts and feelings which interpenetrate them, are filled with the vibrant substance of the universe. Substance is a vital essence, pulsating with life and the desire to express. The substance that comprises your mind, body and affairs constantly seeks to express its life as activity in you and in your world. When allowed to do so consistently through the rhythmic law of giving and receiving, order fills your mind, harmony fills your body and affairs, abundant good fills your world.

If you do not allow the substance of the universe to flow through your mind, body and affairs systematically, you get out of balance with the pulsating rhythm of the universe. Congestion and imbalance follow.

Congestion in the body is always the result of congestion elsewhere, in other departments of your life. By withholding substance, that substance becomes dammed up within you, where it stagnates, spoils and literally poisons your body with ill health.

The remedy?

You have heard it said, "When things get tight, something has to give." *When things get tight, someone has to give! If you have problems of any sort— especially health problems—the "someone" that has to give is you!*

People with health problems are always people who need to give. One authority has estimated that 80 percent of the people who are under the care of physicians, or who are in hospitals, are people who do not know how to give.

These people are trying to receive increased health. *But people who do not know how to give are also people who do not know how to receive.*

That there is a definite connection between illness and poverty has been medically substantiated. Statistics show that the poor get sick more frequently than the well-to-do. They also die younger.

People with health problems are people out of balance. They may have been trying to get more out of life than they have been willing to give to it. They may have been trying to get something for nothing, and are having to pay the high price of ill health. People with health problems are sometimes people who have money or other material possessions, which they are clutching rather than using.

You cannot get something for nothing. You don't have room for it! Unless you give, you have no room to receive.

WITHHOLDING AFFECTS HEALTH

When a person allows his thoughts about money to become stiff, hard, set, unyielding, then his arteries also become stiff, hard, set, unyielding. He is told that he has "hardening of the arteries." *The arteries that hardened first were the main arteries leading to and from his seldom-opened pocketbook!*

People who suffer from problems of constipation are usually people who have a constipated mind and pocketbook. They are holding on to negative memories as well as to money and other material possessions which they should be releasing.

People with weight problems are people who should be giving.

Man often blames his health problems on age, the climate, or heredity, when, in reality, his health problems are the result of his holding on to substance which he should be releasing.

This is a giving universe, as evidenced by the ebb and flow of the tides, by the seasons of the year, by night following day. You cannot cheat this basic law of giving and receiving, which quietly works throughout the universe. It works regardless of your misworking it. You can only cheat yourself out of much health, wealth and happiness when you foolishly try to bypass it.

When you withhold, something is withheld from you. When you do not give, something is taken from you; and that "something" is often your health!

THE SOURCE OF YOUR HEALTH

Perhaps you are indignantly thinking, "Yes, but I do give, and still I am in ill health. I give every cent I can get to pay doctors, druggists and hospital bills. Don't talk to me about giving!"

Giving can heal you if you give voluntarily and consistently, before there is a need, to the constructive experiences of life, rather than giving involuntarily and resentfully, after there is a need, to the destructive experiences of life.

When you give to pay hospital bills, doctors, and meet other pressing expenses, you are not giving voluntarily and consistently to the happy things of life. Instead you are giving involuntarily and resentfully to the negative experiences of life, and your resentment only multiplies your problems. It becomes a vicious circle that gets you nowhere, until you change your attitude and method of giving.

When you begin putting first things first and give constructively to the good things of life, you will find that the destructive experiences lessen and finally disappear so that you no longer have to support them.

HOW TO GIVE FOR HEALTH

How can you invoke a healthy kind of giving that will produce healthy results for you? How can you begin putting first things first in your giving?

Well, what is the first thing to which you should be giving, if you want good health?

You should be giving to the Source of your health, shouldn't you? Giving to the Source of your health gets and keeps you attuned to that Source, and to its constantly renewing, energizing, healing power.

"What or Who is the Source of your health? Who created you?"

"God!"

Not only did He create you, but He has a healthy image of you, since He made you in His own likeness of beauty, wholeness, and life. Scientists state that the universe and everything in it, including man, is composed of energy and nothing but energy. As God's highest creation, you live, move and have your being amid that ceaseless, life-giving energy. If you are not healthy, then it is not God's fault, but your own. You have cut yourself off from the life-giving energy that is within and around you.

It is up to you to make contact again, and when you do, the life current will flow into and through you as renewed health.

How can you give in such a way as to dissolve the block that has short-circuited your health, and again make contact with the divine energy of the universe?

Giving can heal you when you begin to put God, the Source of your health, first financially on a regular, consistent, voluntary basis.

Is this a new idea? Absolutely not! It is one of the oldest secrets for healthy living. Primitive man intuitively knew that he must consistently recognize his Creator as the Source of all his blessings; and primitive man did this by regularly offering sacrifices to his gods in the form of tithes of his crops, cattle, and other financial supply.

Long before Biblical times, the ancient civilizations including the Egyptians, Babylonians, Persians, Arabians, and Chinese knew and practiced tithing a tenth or more of their gross income to their Creator as a form of recognition and appreciation for their blessings.

Why did they give a tithe, ten percent? Because the number "ten" has always been considered the magic number of increase.

The first literal instance of tithing in the Bible occurred in the time of Abraham, when he gave a tithe offering to the High Priest of Salem. In return, Jehovah promised him not only riches, but also protection from the negative experiences of life: "Fear not, I am thy shield and thy exceeding great reward." (Genesis 15:1) There is no evidence of illness in the life of Abraham. He lived a long prosperous life and became the Bible's first historical millionaire. He was so healthy that he fathered a son when he was one hundred years of age and went on to live another seventy-five years.[1]

YOU HAVE TO GIVE ANYWAY

When you recognize God as the Source of your health, and *prove* your recognition and appreciation of that fact by sharing with Him a tenth of all He has

---

1. See chapters 2 and 3 in the author's book, *The Millionaires of Genesis.*

given to you, you release the dammed-up substance within you that has stagnated and poisoned your health. You again become attuned to the rhythmic flow of energy pulsating throughout the universe and increased health is the natural result.

When you withhold God's tenth, you have to give it away—but to the negative experiences of life. You usually have to give many times the amount of your tithe for illness, accidents, family problems, financial and tax problems, loss, fire, theft, legal entanglements, and a thousand and one other ills. Solomon tried to bring this great truth to man's attention when he wrote: "Honor Jehovah with thy substance, and with the first-fruits of all thine increase. So shall thy barns be filled with plenty, and thy vats shall overflow with new wine." (Proverbs 3:9-10) "There is that scattereth, and increaseth yet more; And there is that withholdeth more than is meet, but it tendeth only to want. The liberal soul shall be made fat; And he that watereth shall be watered also himself." (Proverbs 11: 24-25)

There is an old saying, "You will never find a tither in the poorhouse." You won't find him among those crowded into doctor's offices, hospitals or mental institutions either!

I first got acquainted with Mrs. Smith (not her real name) after she had had a serious operation following a freak accident in her home. Bones had been crushed and other serious damage had been done to her body. This was not the first such experience. From her hospital bed, where she lay in casts, heavily bandaged, and in severe pain, she related to me some of her health problems over the years. Along with all the physical pain had come the financial pain of heavy indebtedness resulting from her many illnesses.

This woman had long been a church member, but had given sparingly, thinking she could not afford to give to God, because of large medical bills. It was pointed out that as long as she continued to bow down to the destructive experiences of life, putting them first financially, she would continue to have destructive experiences, for which she would continue to pay a high price. It was suggested that only as she deliberately and immediately began to reverse the process, putting God — Who was the Source of her health — first financially, would the destructive experiences diminish and good health return.

Immediately she began to tithe a tenth of the gross income received by her and her husband. She gave one-half of their monthly tithe to her church, and she gave the other one-half of their monthly tithe to my ministry, where she had learned this spiritual law.

Her physical recovery amazed her physician, who had warned she would probably never walk again. Not only was she soon walking again, but she was also soon free of both crutches and a cane!

Furthermore, after beginning to put God first financially, her husband prospered so in his business that for the first time in years, all her medical bills got paid. This couple has since enjoyed the constructive experiences of life. They redecorated their home and took a vacation — the first in years.

When you do not give in the right way, you give many times that amount in the wrong way. Whereas, when you loosen up and put first things first in your giving, you loosen up and then give up your health problems as well.

A businesswoman recently proved this in an interesting way: After reading *The Prosperity Secrets of the Ages*, she began tithing for financial reasons. Not only were her financial woes soon resolved, but she also "tithed away fifteen pounds" and highly recommends it as a spiritual method for permanently losing weight!

YOUR FAITH IS WHERE YOUR MONEY IS

If you do not give when you have little, you will not give when you have much. In fact, you will never have much to give!

A penny-pinching housewife got very ill with a bronchial infection. She called on a local prayer ministry for healing prayers, but never gave an offering. Instead she excused herself by saying, "My medical bills have been so high I have no money to give." Several weeks later, she telephoned again and complained that no progress had been made. She said, "I have paid the doctors over $300 to heal me of this infection, yet I am as sick as ever."

Remember that you place your faith where you place your money. Your faith is where you are giving. If you cannot afford to give to God in recognition and appreciation of Him as the Source of your health, then you have no faith in Him to heal you, and all the prayers in the world being offered for your healing will be of little permanent benefit. *Your gift indicates your faith. Your lack of a gift indicates your lack of faith.* As Emerson has written: "A man often pays dearly for a small frugality."

CARELESS GIVING RESTRICTS YOUR GOOD

There are those people who complain they are giving their tithes to God's work and still suffer sickness.

These people are often careless in their giving. Such was a widow of seventy-five who had tithed for years to her church. But when her husband died, she neglected to tithe from his estate of $5,000. In a little while she had a bad fall, was in bed for weeks, and continued to suffer ill effects for months.

This illness cost her $500. It was a cheap illness considering the time and treatment involved. Only after she heard a lecture on following the Biblical command to tithe a tenth of all channels of income (Leviticus 27:30–32) did she realize the cause of her illness. She immediately drew out of her savings $500, representing a tithe of her husband's estate, and gave it to her church. She has not been sick since.

Sometimes when folks say they are tithing to God's work, yet still have health problems, there is another reason:

They are giving to God's work at one point, but are receiving spiritual help and inspiration at another point. *You should give at the point or points where you are receiving spiritual help and inspiration.* You would not go to one doctor for treatment, yet pay another. You would not go to one restaurant to be fed, but try to pay at another. So often a person tithes to a certain church or religious organization simply through habit; yet is turning to some spiritual counselor, practitioner, Truth teacher or minister elsewhere for help; often giving nothing or practically nothing in appreciation. This blocks his channel to answered prayer. Remember that gratitude takes three forms: a feeling in the heart, an expression in words, and a *giving in return.*

Beware of indiscriminate giving. *Where* you give of your tithes and offerings to God's work is very important. It may not necessarily be the largest spiritual organization, but rather is that particular individual or organization where you are receiving spiritual help and inspiration.

Many people have the mistaken idea that giving to a needy person is tithing, but it is not. To tithe is to give directly to God's work or workers. The greatest thing you can give a needy person is to introduce him to the spiritual and mental laws of prosperity, which include the act of tithing. As he is taught to look to God as the Source of his supply, rather than looking to people and conditions; and as he proves his faith by putting God first financially through tithing of his "widow's mite," the way always opens for that "mite" to multiply and for him to become permanently prosperous.[2]

Many people have the mistaken idea that giving to relatives is tithing. Often by giving indiscriminately to a relative, you are keeping him from developing his own talents and abilities, which would lead to his prosperity. The one being helped financially comes to resent such help, since he feels obligated. Innately he knows he should be developing his own abilities rather than sponging off those of another.

If you wish to help those about you, do not use your tithe for that purpose. In Bible times the tithe went always to the priests and temples, to those in the Lord's work. It was "holy unto Jehovah." (Leviticus 27:30) The rule still applies.

A businessman had been debating whether to tithe or to use that money to pay for his daughter's psychiatric treatment. When he realized that tithing to God's

---

2. See the chapter, "The Prosperous Mite, One of the World's Mightiest Financial Transactions" in the author's book, *The Millionaire from Nazareth*.

work had nothing to do with his daughter's financial affairs, he stopped paying her bills, and began tithing a tenth of his gross income to the organization where he had learned about the tithing law.

It was then that his daughter did what her psychiatrist had been urging her to do for her own healing: she went to work and began paying her own bills. Her job proved to be perfect therapy. Soon she needed no more expensive treatments and she was happily on the way to independent prosperity as well.

ATTITUDE AS IMPORTANT AS GIFT

However, your attitude toward giving to the minister or church that is inspiring you is just as important as your actual tithe.

A businessman with a chronic heart condition had spent hundreds of dollars for medical treatment. At the same time, he was regularly seeing his minister, asking for spiritual treatment for his health. This sick man thought nothing of paying hundreds of dollars for medical treatment for his health problems. He also employed one of the most expensive lawyers in town to handle his various business problems and thought nothing of paying his high fees. Yet this same businessman bitterly complained because his minister (whose prayers he hoped could heal him) was paid a good salary, and was provided with a car and house by his congregation.

This businessman considered himself a Christian follower of Jesus Christ. Yet he overlooked the great Truth that a person who could turn water into wine, multiply bread and fish at will, raise the dead to life and heal all disease, could hardly be counted poor. Such a person today would be considered a millionaire![3]

To be a true Christian, a follower of Jesus Christ, is to follow His example and to be at one with all interior and exterior wealth. You do not honor the rich Creator of this lavish universe through poverty, and neither does your minister!

It is your spiritual duty to do all that you can to prosper the minister, counselor, practitioner, or Truth teacher who is inspiring you and praying for your healing. If for no other reason than to safeguard your own best interests, you should make your chosen channel of spiritual inspiration as prosperous as possible.

However, there are other reasons for doing so:

The world in these times wants and needs ministers, spiritual counselors and teachers of Truth who can not only tell you how to be prosperous and healthy, but who through their own lives are proving that they know spiritual laws, just as Jesus proved them. The world loves, respects and listens to those in spiritual work who have proved the spiritual laws of prosperity and healing. Such ministers and teachers have a high-powered spiritual consciousness that draws and inspires a large and loyal following, just as Jesus drew and inspired a large following.

You open the way for the improvement of your own health when you support financially, as well as spiritually, such a minister, counselor or Truth teacher. Not only do your gifts help free that one from material worries, so that he (or she) is freer to minister more

---

3. See chapter "From Carpenter to Lord of Plenty" in the author's book, *The Millionaire from Nazareth.*

fully on the spiritual plane. But by giving to such a one, you tune in on his healthy, prosperous spiritual consciousness, and you receive a blessing of expanded good in your own life.

Perhaps you say, "I do not give money to those who spiritually inspire me, but I do show my appreciation with gifts." Would you take your doctor or lawyer a gift instead of paying him properly for services rendered? Your minister or counselor has to eat, pay taxes, and educate his children, too!

There are people everywhere who are Christians only up to their hip pockets. They give the Lord practically everything: advice, excuses, good intentions, a little time and even a little energy—everything except the coin of the realm. Giving your minister or church money is no less spiritual than giving them your thoughts, prayers, time or talents. Money is spiritual too! The Old Testament prophet pointed out: "The silver is mine, and the gold is mine, saith the Lord of hosts." (Haggai 2:8) The prominent engineering genius, R. G. LeTourneau, who became a multimillionaire through tithing put it bluntly, "It is all right to give God credit, but He can also use cash!"

SEEK HELP REGARDLESS

If you do not have a tithe offering or gift of money to offer when you seek spiritual help, do not hesitate to ask for the help needed. But do not hesitate to open the way mentally for a gift of money to come to you, which you will pass on to the one offering help. Say honestly, "I do not have a gift of money to give in appreciation for your help now, but I will have soon."

A sick housewife once asked a spiritual counselor to visit her at home to talk and pray with her for healing of a chronic condition that specialized treatment had not healed. When the counselor arrived, the sick woman explained she had no money but that she would soon have some. Together they talked and prayed. The counselor pointed out certain attitudes of bitterness, resentment and unforgiveness that needed to be released; that visit proved to be the turning point toward healing for this long-suffering woman.

Within a week the counselor received a letter from this woman who wrote, "Although I did not have an offering for you, I knew I would have if I opened my mind to receive it. Within a few days after your visit, I received an unexpected gift of $100, and am happy to share with you my tithe of $10."

If you have the money, however, don't wait until you have been healed to render your offering. *To delay your gift can delay your healing.* So often people ignorantly say, "When I have been helped, *then* I will give an offering." Such an attitude of doubt interferes with healing.

Just as you pay a doctor upon completion of an office call, before there is any way of knowing whether his treatment has healed you — in like manner, you should give at least a token offering to a spiritual counselor, teacher or minister when you ask for help, before you know whether his treatment has helped you.

Your gift is an act of faith that opens the way for the spiritual help rendered to aid you; whereas if you do not give, you have not opened the way in faith to receive your healing. No matter how powerful the spiritual treatment, it often has little lasting effect.

The Hebrews of old fully understood and applied this spiritual law of giving first, *before* there was any sign of answered prayer. Over and over they would pray to God for help, and then immediately they would offer a sacrifice to Him, in anticipation and appreciation of answered prayer. Their sacrifices were always of a financial nature, usually consisting of their finest cattle. It is still an Eastern custom that when people ask the help of a healer or prophet, an offering is always given. The people of the East would not think of visiting a holy man or shrine without taking along an offering. They consider it an act of faith, as well as an act of spiritual worship, to give. Also, they always return with "thank offerings" when a life has been saved, a healing has occurred, a prosperity demonstration manifested, or when in some other way a prayer has been answered. The act of giving both *before* and *after* answered prayer is a practice that has predominated in the East since ancient times.[4]

GIFT WITH STRINGS IS UNHEALTHY

However, in this matter of giving, beware of giving unless you can give freely. A gift that is given with strings attached is an unhealthy gift. It is not a gift but a bribe. And it brings unhappy results, often in the form of ill health.

A woman who was dangerously overweight, out of harmony with her daughter, and having dire financial problems, claimed she had been using the mental and spiritual laws for successful living, to no avail. It was suggested that she give, if she wished to receive, since

---

4. See the chapters "The Prosperity Law of Opulence" and "The Miracle Law of Prosperity" in the author's book, *The Millionaire Moses.*

right thought always leads to right action.

One night when I lectured in her area, she introduced herself, saying: "See this nice church? I gave those lovely stained glass windows, but the new minister has made some changes of which I disapprove, so I am asking that the windows be returned to me." It is little wonder that woman had so many problems.

A respected church member, who was known as a generous giver, began to have trouble with his right shoulder, arm and hand. His shoulder was filled with a mysterious pain, which doctors were unable to cure. His right arm and hand would get so numb that he was afraid to drive his car, play golf, or participate in other normal activities requiring their use.

After months of medical tests and various treatments, which revealed nothing, this man talked with his minister. Knowing the power of attitudes to affect the body, his minister immediately recognized the cause of his mysterious ailment.

Though this man had often given large sums of money to his church, he had always stipulated how his money was to be spent. The minister bravely pointed out that he must financially release his gifts; that he had been mentally holding to them, as evidenced by the trouble in his shoulder, arm, hand. Being conscientious in his desire to give, this fine businessman immediately realized his mistake, and stopped dictating how his tithes were to be used. As his attitudes returned to normal, so did his health.

OTHER WAYS THAT GIVING CAN HEAL

Along with the formal act of giving systematically to God, the Source of your health, there are other acts of giving that can heal you.

Pay your doctor! To cheat your doctor out of his fees is to cheat yourself out of good health. Giving to your doctor can heal you.

If you do not pay your doctor for his services rendered in past illnesses, then his resentment toward you coupled with your own sense of guilt and obligation, can keep you mentally tied to him and to past illness. Such an emotional link can cause you ill health in the present and future. As Emerson has written: "Always pay; for first or last you must pay your entire debt." So forgive, give up resentment toward, and pay all past medical bills, if you want to go free to good health in the present and future.

Improved health can actually be withheld until order and harmony are first established concerning past financial obligations. I recently talked with a couple who were heavily in debt and suffering from severe health problems. The basic cause of their many problems was finally revealed: A deep resentment toward a large medical bill of the past, which they had refused to pay. *Basically there is only one disease, congestion. And there is only one cure, circulation.*

Another way that giving can heal you is by forming a vacuum. Get rid of old things you no longer use. Clean up and clean out the closets, files, desk, kitchen cabinets, lock boxes at the bank, glove compartment and trunk in the car. Get rid of what you do not want to make room for what you do want.

In *The Dynamic Laws of Prosperity* is the story of a lady who had tried unsuccessfully to lose weight. Learning of the vacuum law, she realized she had stored up many unused possessions in the cellar and closets, as well as cramming her home with unnecessary objects. She fearlessly called in the Salvation

Army and passed on all unused items that could do good elsewhere. Thereafter, for the first time she lost weight and maintained that loss.

There is a mental correspondence: *When you give away old things, you unconsciously give away old problems. When you give away valued things, you unconsciously give away expensive problems.*

Make it a point to give in all the usual ways. Unhealthy people are self-centered people who are clutching their health problems to them. Giving helps them to think about and help others, which is fine therapy for freedom from their own ills.

Give of your time, talents, substance. Give of your friendship and love. Give kind words of praise and appreciation. Say often to those nearest you, "I love you and I think you're wonderful." Say to the downhearted, "You can succeed. You have what it takes!" Silently praise yourself, too, since self-condemnation can cause ill health.

Write notes, send cards for all occasions, give flowers, candy, books, records, other lovely gifts. It takes so little to make other people happy; often it is the little acts of kindness which cost the least that mean the most to others, and which, in turn, aid your own health.

Above all, show deliberate appreciation in some way to all your benefactors from the past, whether they be relatives, friends, or business associates that are now near or far. If they have passed from this earth plane, give in memory of them. By doing so, you pay an old emotional debt to them which frees you for new blessings.

In all these ways, as well as in others that will be revealed, you will have a delightful, exciting, satisfying time proving that your giving can heal you!

A SPECIAL NOTE FROM THE AUTHOR

Through the generous outpouring of their tithes over the years, the readers of my books have helped me to financially establish three new ministries, the most recent being the nondenominational *UNITY WORLDWIDE* with global headquarters in Palm Desert, California. Many thanks for your help in the past, and for all that you continue to share.

You are also invited to share your tithes with the churches of your choice, especially those which teach the truths stressed in this book. Such churches include the metaphysical churches of Unity, Religious Science, Divine Science, Science of Mind, and other related churches, many of which are members of the International New Thought Movement. (For a list of such churches write The International New Thought Alliance, 7314 E. Stetson Drive, Scottsdale, AZ 85251.) Your support of such churches can help spread the Truth that mankind is now seeking in this New Age of metaphysical enlightenment.

NOTE: For further information on the success power of giving, see additional material in the author's other books, specifically: *The Dynamic Laws of Prosperity, The Prosperity Secrets of the Ages, Open Your Mind to Prosperity, Open Your Mind to Receive*; and the "Millionaires of the Bible" series.

Conclusion . . . .

THE AUTHOR'S FINAL WORDS
TO YOU:
Can You Accept Your Healing?

There are people who read books such as this one that say, "It all sounds fine but it doesn't work for me." They add almost triumphantly, "I have used these healing techniques and I am as sick as ever!"

Of those who sought Him out for healing Jesus often implied, "Do you want to be healed?" He knew that God can only do for you what He can first do through you—and through your mental attitudes.

Life demands much of the healthy person. He is expected to get up each morning and do a full day's work. He is expected to assume a full share of the responsibilities that go with meeting life victoriously. As every physician knows, much that passes for disease is an attempt to escape life's responsibilities. Such people "enjoy" ill health and dare anyone to heal them.

Perhaps you've heard the story about the long-suffering lady who began to use the mental and spiritual laws of healing, and her health quickly improved. People began to say, "How well you look." One day when another friend had just made this "disturbing" comment, the woman snorted, "I am not as well as you think," and she went back to bed.

Psychologists say that you can have anything that you can mentally accept, but you have to mentally accept it first. Psychologists also say that when you think you have been rejected, you are in for shock. The good you desire never rejects you—you have subconsciously rejected it! You reject healing when you hang on emotionally to illness and to the attention and sympathy that accompany it.

Health or sickness, the choice is up to you. As Jehovah pointed out to Moses and the Children of Israel so long ago: "I have set before thee life and and death, the blessing and the curse; therefore choose life, that thou mayest live." (Deuteronomy 30:19)

As you use often the healing techniques described in this book along with whatever medical, psychiatric or chiropractic help that seems best, then go one step further. Invoke the healing law of mental acceptance by affirming often: "LORD, I AM READY! I AM READY TO ACCEPT MY COMPLETE HEALING IN MIND, BODY, AFFAIRS AND RELATIONSHIPS. LORD, I DO ACCEPT MY COMPLETE HEALING NOW." Then ask your Creator to reveal just which of the healing laws is most applicable to your condition. The ones that interest, inspire and fascinate you most are usually the ones that contain the greatest healing power for you.

When you discover them, get busy consistently using them. Don't be like the impatient lady who wrote about another of my books, "I have read your book all the way through but nothing has happened." In many instances of healing, Jesus directed the sufferer to do certain things for himself; and it was only after he made the effort to follow Jesus' instruction that healing occurred. So read and then *do!*

As you follow through by doing your part, in due time the Master's promise can doubtless apply to you: "Go thy way; thy faith hath made thee whole." (Mark 10:52)